MODERNITY, RELIGION, AND THE WAR ON TERROR

The war on terror cannot be truly understood without investigating the legitimacy of modernity, the challenge that religion presents to modernization, the inescapable conflicts attending the emergence and expansion of modernity, and the post-colonial predicament from which Islamist reaction arises. Richard Dien Winfield illuminates the war on terror in light of these issues, presenting an anti-foundationalist justification of the rationality and freedom of modernity, while assessing how religion can stand in opposition to modernity and why Islam has been a privileged vehicle of anti-modern religious revolt.

Winfield shows that the privatization that religion must undergo to be compatible with modern freedom involves no capitulation to relativism, but rather is a theological imperative on which the truth of religion depends. Exposing the limits of any purely secular modernization of Islam, Winfield shows how Islam can draw upon its core tradition to repudiate the oppression of Islamist reaction and become at home in the modern world.

To Louis Dupré

Modernity, Religion, and the War on Terror

RICHARD DIEN WINFIELD
University of Georgia, USA

ASHGATE

Published by
Ashgate Publishing Limited
Gower House
Croft Road
Aldershot
Hampshire GU11 3HR
England

Ashgate Publishing Company
Suite 420
101 Cherry Street
Burlington, VT 05401-4405
USA

Ashgate website: http://www.ashgate.com

British Library Cataloguing in Publication Data
Winfield, Richard Dien, 1950–
   Modernity, religion, and the war on terror
   1. Religion and civilization 2. Civilization, Modern – 21st century 3. Islam and secularism
   4. Islamic fundamentalism 5. Terrorism – Religious aspects – Islam 6. World politics – 21st
   century 7. Islamic countries – Civilization – Western influences 8. Islamic countries – Social
   conditions
   I. Title
   201.6'9

Library of Congress Cataloging-in-Publication Data
Winfield, Richard Dien, 1950–
   Modernity, religion, and the War on Terror/Richard Dien Winfield.
      p. cm.
   Includes index.
   ISBN-13: 978-0-7546-6056-9 (hardcover: alk. paper) 1. Religion and culture. 2. Civilization,
   Modern. 3. Islam. 4. Terrorism. I. Title.
   BL65.C8W56 2007
   201'.7–dc22

2007004391

ISBN 978-0-7546-6056-9

Printed and bound in Great Britain by TJ International Ltd, Padstow, Cornwall.

Contents

Acknowledgments

The following work grew out of an essay, "Modernity, Religion, and the War on Terrorism", published in *International Readings on Theory, History and Philosophy of Culture*, 18, 2004, pp. 329–47, after being delivered in October 2003 at the 6th International Congress in Philosophy and Culture in St Petersburg, Russia.

Chapters 1 and 2 incorporate with modifications and additions material first published as Chapter 18, "Modernity and the Recovery of Truth, Right and Beauty", of Richard Dien Winfield, *Autonomy and Normativity: Investigations of Truth, Right and Beauty* (London: Ashgate, 2001), pp. 227–44.

Chapter 4 incorporates with modifications and additions material first published as "Post-Colonialism and Right", in *Beyond Liberalism and Communitarianism: Studies in Hegel's* Philosophy of Right, edited by Robert Williams (Albany: State University of New York Press, 2001), pp. 91–109.

The publishers are thanked for their permission to incorporate the above material.

Introduction

Ever since the Islamist mass murders of 9/11, the war on terrorism has become a central preoccupation of the new world order. Yet as the battle gains increasing attention, confusion still reigns as to the true identity of its antagonists and the fundamental nature of the conflict.

The very slogan of the struggle invites perplexity. Is "the war on terrorism" really a war, and, even if it is, does it really combat "terrorism" without qualification?

Certainly "the war on terrorism" is not a war in any conventional sense. It does involve armed conflict between nations as well as civil warfare within others whenever the "terrorists" enlist governments in their support or directly fight for political power. Yet, the conflict equally extends beyond battlefields and national frontiers. To pursue shadowy conspirators who commit criminal outrages against civilians without using any territorial base, what must be undertaken are international police actions, rather than military campaigns. And with the "terrorist enemy" enlisting new recruits from populations dispersed across the globe, victory can hardly be imagined without the mobilization of non-coercive resources, both secular and religious.

However the "war" proceeds, it is certainly not being waged against terrorism in general. Terrorists all perpetrate inexcusable crimes against humanity by expressly targeting civilians for kidnap, torture, and murder, and by putting whole non-combatant populations under fear of indiscriminate attack. Terrorists may claim that no other options are possible against the evils they combat, either because they are too weak to confront military targets, or because they lack the mass support to wage non-violent protests, boycotts, general strikes, and political campaigns, or because they face regimes so pervasively oppressive as to preclude any peaceful mass actions. Yet these arguments cannot hide the truth that terrorism is a deliberate strategy undertaken because its perpetrators decide to trample upon the human rights of civilians and make indiscriminate murder the means to their ends.[1] For this reason,

---

1 Michael Walzer provides a powerful development of these arguments against today's apologists for terror in "Terrorism: A Critique of Excuses" in Michael Walzer, *Arguing about War* (New Haven: Yale University Press, 2004), pp. 51–66.

all terrorist groups deserve to be brought to justice, with prosecution of not just the actual murderers, but their leaders, fellow conspirators, and other abettors as well. Nonetheless, the war on terrorism is not directed at all those movements that have used terror to advance local struggles for national emancipation. Groups like the Front de Libération Nationale (FLN) in Algeria, the Palestinian Liberation Organization, the Irish Republican Army, the Basque separatists, and the Tamil Tigers of Sri Lanka have all targeted civilians to achieve goals revolving around some form of political independence. Yet due to the regional limits of their goals, none of these movements present the world challenge that the war on terrorism addresses. Despite its indiscriminate reference to terrorism, what that war fights are not all groups conspiring to attack officials and civilians of targeted regimes, nor all governments sponsoring such groups or terrorizing their own subjects.

The enemy instead is a specific movement of Islamist religious warriors. Far from being destructive nihilists killing without purpose,[2] they are waging holy war to purge infidels from the territories dominated by their creed, there impose religious rule over political, social, family, and cultural affairs, and assault secular nations resisting their struggle. These Jihadists might thereby seem to have a merely regional agenda, like the movements that have used terror to promote national independence and political separatism. Moreover, the Islamist warriors' goal of establishing religious rule might seem to make them little different than religious zealots clinging to Christianity, Hinduism, and Judaism, who have violently attacked secular institutions and opposing religious groups. Yet, there is a fundamental difference on both scores that underlies why the war on terrorism combats none of these other movements, be they secular or religious. Islamist Jihadists are the enemy of the war on terrorism both because their aims extend beyond any merely regional agenda and because their opposition to secular freedoms is more far reaching than that of any other contemporary fundamentalist movements.

---

2   Post-modernists, like their would-be critic, Alain Badiou, may be apt to view 9/11 and its aftermath as nothing but "bloody and nihilistic games of power without purpose and without truth", but the reduction of the conflict to another exercise of the will to power ignores how their own diagnosis can be more than an ideological power play, as well as the most obvious features of the struggle. See Alain Badiou, *Infinite Thought: Truth and the Return of Philosophy* (London: Continuum, 2004), p. 160.

The Islamist agenda may well focus upon bringing an authentic Islamic community to the nations that are currently majority Muslim and removing infidels from the territories most holy and significant for Islamic tradition—the Arabian Peninsula, Palestine, and the Fertile Crescent. These regional struggles, however, hardly exhaust the ambitions of Islamist Jihad. Because Islam, unlike Judaism, does not restrict its message to a chosen people, but regards the worldwide spread of the Prophet's teaching as a religious imperative, Islamists have very global aspirations. Moreover, Islamists seek to renew the long tradition of the Caliphate, first established by Muhammad's immediate seventh-century successors and only abolished in 1924 by the modernizing Turkish revolutionary, Mustafa Kemal, the Atatürk. Under the Caliphate, political rule and religious authority are joined and holy law reigns supreme over all spheres of life. Reestablishing this empire of faith is the Islamist dream. Because the traditions of Jews, Hindus, and Christians all distinguish religious authority from political power, their "fundamentalists" have something far less inclusive in mind. By contrast, the global hegemonic aims of Islamist Jihad directly challenge any regimes that uphold secular law and the rights of self-government, civil society, and an emancipated household, all of which recognize freedoms indifferent to sacred legality and religious affiliation.

These signal features decisively frame the identity of the predominant protagonist in the war on terrorism. An international coalition may have been enlisted to wage the war with greatest effect and cooperation, but it is the United States that is both preeminent foreign victim of and preeminent force battling the enemy movement.

The central role of the United States would be contingent if all it rested upon were the immediate objects of Islamist ire on the threshold of 9/11: American toleration of Israeli occupation of Gaza and the West Bank, the stationing of American troops in Saudi Arabia, and United States support for the United Nations sanctions on Iraq. Each of these foreign policies could have been rescinded in accord with the principles of freedom to which the United States appeals in legitimating its institutions, without removing the enduring antagonism.

To be consistent, American Middle East policy must abide by the democratic proviso that rational agents not be deprived of participation in self-government. This right to political freedom neither restricts political autonomy to ethnically defined peoples, nor gives each such people a right to self-determination. Although the right of a people to self-determination has been raised as a banner of emancipation by such unhappy bedfellows as Woodrow Wilson, Lenin, and Hitler, it provides a recipe for imperiling the political rights of minorities and setting the stage for ethnic cleansing. Once the unit of self-government is restricted to any culturally defined group, inhabitants with a different background face the stark choice of staying in a country from whose governance they are excluded or relocating with their ethnic compatriots to some other territory from which all others are politically disempowered. As the United States exhibits, a democracy need not be a nation-state, where citizenship and ethnic identity are joined. Indeed, to be consistent with political freedom, a self-governing citizenry must be defined by adherence to a common constitution, rather than by cultural unities given independently of political association. This principle for defining the unit of self-government enables Palestinians to gain their political freedom in whatever body politic they can join in as democratic equals. Only because the Israeli government refuses to grant them full citizenship in a greater Israel and Palestinians remain largely unwilling to join Israelis as fellow citizens in a democratic binational state, can the two-state option be a legitimate alternative, offering the most feasible accord with the same principles of self-government to which the United States subscribes. Accordingly, the United States could have ceased tolerating Israel's refusal to grant full independence to Gaza and the West Bank, including East Jerusalem, while insuring Israeli democracy's territorial security, without compromising America's own institutions and professed principles.

The same consistency to democratic principle could just as well have been fulfilled by more promptly ending the stationing of American forces in the Arabian Peninsula and withdrawing United States support of the United Nations embargos on Iraqi trade. Although the Arabian nations that hosted American troops at least formally agreed to their presence, as deterrence against Iraqi aggression, the forces could have been withdrawn earlier without undermining freedom in the United States or further deepening oppression in the Arabian Peninsula. Similarly, even though the hardship of the Iraqi civilian population under the United Nations embargos had no small connection to the ruinous foreign adventures and domestic tyranny of Saddam Hussein, the United States could have consistently supported removing some, if not all, trade sanctions as ineffective instruments for diminishing Iraq's threat to the freedoms, however limited they may be, of its neighbors and its own peoples.

If the terrorist movement advocated these specific changes in the name of making United States foreign policy consistent with America's own principles of freedom, there would be no intractable conflict.

The two sides of the war on terrorism could reconcile themselves through the avenues of political liberalism, which insists on parties respecting each other's legitimacy and coming to an understanding on how their shared normative commitments could be made more consistent with themselves.

The Islamists waging holy war do not, however, oppose American foreign policy in the Middle East for its inconsistency. Bringing self-government to the Palestinians is not their aim. It is instead to erect an Islamic state extending over all Palestine from which infidels would be expelled and excluded, and under which Palestinians would submit to their clerical masters. Similarly, the Islamists demanded an end to the embargos against Iraq not in respect of the universal rights of Iraqi civilians, but in defense of Muslims against the pressures of infidels. Analogously, the withdrawal of American forces from the Arabian Peninsula has been demanded not in defense of the secular autonomies of political and social independence, but to cleanse holy Islamic territories of the pollution of non-Muslim warriors and diminish the influence of infidel power over the Arab Islamic heartland. And more recently, the Jihad against the American occupation of Iraq has aimed at not the establishment of self-government and civil and household emancipation, but rather the imposition of Islamist rule over the Fertile Crescent.

On these terms, any reconciliation is precluded. Even if the United States were to revise its policies in the Middle East to comply with the Islamist agenda, America would still comprise the greatest enemy Islamist militancy faces, an enemy whose very existence is intolerable for the Muslim zealot. What makes the United States the most formidable challenge to holy warriors is not just that America is the most economically dynamic, militarily powerful, politically resilient, and culturally influential threat to Islamist hegemony. It is rather that the United States stands as the greatest bulwark of the project of civilization that distinguishes modernity from all other historical forms of life. Modern times have been ravaged by an unmatched carnage between conflicting world views. Yet, one has emerged whose agenda calls into question all given traditions, demanding that what counts as valid in theory and practice be sanctioned by an autonomous reason, emancipated from all prevailing dogma and recognizing conduct to be legitimate only once it has overthrown the hold of given convention and enacted the system of institutions giving freedom reality. All other civilizational projects encumber reason and conduct with privileged foundations, whose given character leaves thought and action conditioned by some particular ground, whose authority can always be questioned. By setting reason and conduct free from tradition and embracing rational autonomy, modernity advocates practices that possess universality precisely because their self-determined character liberates them of dependence upon any external, particular conditions. For this reason, the modern institutions of freedom have an inherently global reach and authority in contrast to pre-modern formations, whose attachment to particular roots makes their global expansion problematic. Unlike other forms of community, those of modernity have legitimacy independent of any foundations. Just this allows for their philosophical defense without appeal to the pragmatic assumptions of political liberalism, which can offer no answer to those who do not share its moral intuitions.

The history of the United States brings into the sharpest relief all the normative struggles that attend the rise of modern institutions of freedom. On the one hand, the United States has been riven with the challenges internal remnants of pre-modern practices pose to any emergent system of freedom. Slavery and the persistence of racism, both legal and private, have had to be combated to realize the universal rights of property, moral accountability, family membership, civil society, and self-government. Lifting the oppression of women in the household, in society, and in politics has been an equally abiding task, only partially fulfilled by the reform of family law in line with marital equality, the enforcement of equal opportunity for all genders in the economy, and the granting of women's suffrage. Similarly, the campaigns for gay rights and freeing marriage and parenting from restriction to heterosexual unions present another chapter in the distinctly modern agenda of removing all obstacles to bringing conduct into accord with self-determination. And the ongoing campaigns to secure equal economic opportunity through regulation of market relations, to ensure that civil and political affairs accommodate family responsibilities so that household roles do not jeopardize social and political opportunity, and to prevent economic and other social power from subverting political equality all reflect the endemic domestic challenge of making society fully civil and keeping civil society in proper harmony with household emancipation and self-government.

Just as the trajectories of American domestic history are circumscribed by these imperatives for overcoming internal impediments to modernity's institutions of freedom, so the history of the United States' external relations exhibit the problems of keeping an emergent modern state true to the agenda of freedom in its relations with pre-modern regimes, regimes being modernized from without, and post-modern foreign enemies. The wars against Native Americans and their subsequent internment in a reservation system have been marked by the same pre-modern racism and ethnic chauvinism that have imperiled domestic freedom. Yet they equally reflect the unavoidable conflict between the modern state and traditional communities ordered by kinship and other hierarchies incompatible with the universal rights of the system of freedom. Similarly, the late entry of the United States into colonial conquest and its subsequent withdrawal from most possessions exhibit the temptations of self-serving imperial exploitation. Also, however, they manifest the dilemma of how to modernize oppressive communities without subverting the sought after institutions of freedom, whose own community requires free participation by those upon whom it is imposed. Although the United States has supported many a regime that violates political, social, and household rights, aided in the suppression of opposition movements seeking to realize the freedoms of modernity, and promoted global economic policies favoring American corporate wealth at the expense of more equitable international development, none of these foreign transgressions of its own principles of freedom would make the United States the focal enemy of Islamist militancy. Already, Europe, Japan, India, China, and the other Asian Tigers together possess greater economic clout and are even more dependent on Middle Eastern oil and the good will of the autocratic and corrupt regimes that repine atop their seas of petroleum. If the United States were just another imperial colossus, projecting its influence in the tradition of every world power before it, holy war could just as well proceed on its peripheries, confronting lesser powers who are all the more oppressive.

Yet, for all its history of internal and external transgressions, the United States has figured for almost a century as the greatest pillar of family emancipation, civil society, self-government, and cultural freedom, playing the central role in defeating the totalitarian challenges to the existence and further globalization of modernity. These challenges contested modern principles of right on very different grounds from those setting pre-modern traditionalists against the institutions of freedom.

Marxist-Leninist regimes and movements, on the one hand, have contested the universal claims of civil society and self-government, regarding each as a tool with which the particular social interest of capital exercises hegemony. So long as free enterprise persists, they have maintained, economic inequality cannot be remedied and no degree of universal suffrage and freedom of speech and political association can prevent the concentration of wealth from politically privileging corporations, rendering democracy a bourgeois oligarchy in which corporate power dominates the state. Certainly, these are problems that must be resolved for society to be civil and politics to be free of social domination. Yet, the solution offered by the communist dictatorships in the name of the proletariat has only collapsed the demarcation of state and society, substituting state management of the economy for the achievement of equal economic opportunity while substituting domination by a particular self-appointed vanguard for social autonomy and self-government.

By contrast, Nazi and Fascist regimes have repudiated the universality of modern rights by promoting the hegemony of a particular ethnically defined people, immediately embodied in the unrestrained will of a leader. Although their repudiation of modernity gets couched in terms of pseudo-scientific arguments of racial superiority, their most powerful ideological support is provided by the post-modern diagnosis of rationality as will to power. On this grand narrative, normative claims in theory and practice always proceed from historically contingent foundations, which therefore are insusceptible of any unqualified justification. Action and thinking are thus endemically heteronomous, always determined from without, always incapable of breaking free from the hold of arbitrary practice. This leaves no escape from the dilemmas of foundationalism, which afflict justification so long as what allegedly possesses validity remains distinguished from what confers validity. This distinction leaves the privileged foundation of justification always suspect, insofar as it can never meet its own standard of legitimation. Because that standard makes justification consist in being derived from the privileged foundation, that foundation will only be valid if it derive from, rather than be, the privileged source of validity. Yet, in order to be sanctioned in the same way that it sanctions everything else, the foundation must be determined by itself. In that case, however, it ceases to be a privileged given, antecedent to what it endows with validity. Moreover, then what it is to be valid ceases to be something determined by some prior ground. Instead, the distinction between source and recipient of justification collapses, undermining foundationalism at the very moment that it strives to be self-referentially consistent.

So long as justification remains identified with foundationalism, however, every normative claim consists in an attempt to impose particular values upon all. Because these values rest on some foundation that cannot be legitimated without subverting foundational justification, they may be advanced as if possessing universal validity, but they remain arbitrary. Hence, values are forwarded ultimately because their advocate chooses to foist them upon others in what amounts to a play for power.

Value positing is a grab for power precisely because values lay claim to universal validity, yet on this diagnosis have no other basis than the choice of whoever affirms them. They presume to bind all, but only serve the particular will that arbitrarily advances them.

Although every value system will thereby be an instance of a will to power, this does not provide justification for neutrality towards all values, as the closet liberals among post-modernists would like to believe. Since not all value systems are tolerant of others, value neutrality is itself a particular standpoint, whose claims of universal validity should be just as bogus as any other. Instead of sanctioning tolerance, the alleged contingent foundations of all norms leaves one value system uniquely consistent: that which imposes its norms as nothing other than particular values rooted in the will of its advocates, who make their bid for hegemony without masking the arbitrary particularity of their efforts. Only such a position casts aside the veiled deception of advancing the preference of a particular will as if it commanded universal validity. This recipe for a new aristocracy of world conquerors, who seek domination for their particular values, is the guiding principle giving fascism its strongest rationale against the freedoms of modernity.

In securing the defeat of fascism in World War II and in containing and facilitating the collapse of Stalin and his heirs, the United States has emerged as the single most crucial representative of the civilizational project of modernity, even if it may still lag in fully realizing equal household, social, and political opportunity. For its part, among all contemporary religions, Islam contains the most widespread and dangerous anti-modern movement.

These facts raise two general questions. To begin with, how can religion stand in opposition to modernity? Secondly, what is it about Islam that allows it to be a privileged vehicle for anti-modern terrorism? In order to answer both these questions in their full significance, one must first consider the essential character of modernity with respect to its normativity and then examine modernity's relation to the different spheres of culture, paying special attention to religion. Next, one must investigate the inescapable tensions that attend the emergence and expansion of modernity. Only then, can the true import of the "war on terrorism" be understood.

Chapter 1

Modernity and Foundations

If modernity were merely a historical period, it would not be susceptible of philosophical treatment. Reduced to a fact of convention, modernity would be as contingent as any practice, which, as an engagement of will, can always be other than it is. To apprehend the modern age as it exists, reason would have to yield to historical reflection, subject to all the limitations of empirical investigation. Modernity, however, is not equivalent to all the givens of recent history. Although it may have emerged in the present epoch, modernity has done so as a contested agenda, realized to varying degrees in different regions. Whatever actualization it may have won, modernity is a normative project, aiming to establish a civilization in which rational autonomy can be at home. For that reason, modernity is subject to philosophical evaluation.

Increasingly, any philosophical defense of modernity has been called into question by a wholesale attack on the perennial hallmarks of humanity's triumph over meaningless contingency: truth, right, beauty, and faith. Instead of representing the universal, unconditioned measures of knowledge, conduct, art, and piety, truth, right, beauty, and faith have been reduced to meaning, value, taste, and conviction, factors relative to particular historical conventions as contingent as any ideals they ground. Cognition, action, artistry, and religion are denied the autonomy to provide universally valid achievements, untainted by particular conditions. Condemned to dependency upon historically relative practices, the search for truth, the quest for justice, the striving after beauty, and the turn to the divine either capitulate to the reigning tradition of some local community or revel in their own arbitrariness, imposing openly particular values in exercise of a will to power. The future is made hostage to the past as science, conduct, art, and worship bow to common usage or to the bare stipulation of a historically relative self. Yet because cognition is left conditioned by contingent convention, the past forfeits its own objectivity, ceasing to be a topic for impartial understanding and becoming instead an instrument for strategic use, recast according to pragmatic plans for the future.

Modernity, Foundations, and Normativity

Can modernity counter these challenges and uphold its defining promise to break with arbitrary convention and still provide a life worth living? In departure from all other forms of civilization, modernity advances the project of erecting a way of life in which nothing can count as legitimate unless it is sanctioned by reason. Tradition, roots, kinship, faith, and every other given relationship are called into question. All norms—practical, theoretical, artistic, and theological—must first be justified by rational inquiry to warrant compliance. Accordingly, reason must free itself of obedience to external authority, be it sacred or profane, and escape bondage to dogmas whose immunity from examination leaves everything based upon them relative to unjustified assertions. Unless reason can be autonomous, it can hardly be its own judge and achieve the self-legitimation on which reason's own sovereign role depends. Not surprisingly, by placing the autonomy of reason at the pinnacle of authority, modernity ends up extending legitimacy to no other conventions than institutions of freedom. Whether in the household, in society, or in politics, the only practices that modernity recognizes to conform to rational autonomy are those that provide some mode of self-determination.

In face of reigning tradition, the birth of the modern therefore calls for liberating the future from the past. If right is to prevail and right is the reality of freedom sanctioned by reason, the habits of the past must have no irrevocable hold upon what is to be done. Yet if reason has authority in virtue of its own autonomy and the autonomy of reason is not an empty flight from the given but the fountain of truth, then the past must be liberated from the future, as a reality fit for impartial comprehension independently of any pragmatic aims. Modernity's task is not to forsake comprehending reality in favor of transforming it. The challenge of the modern spirit is to secure objective knowledge and to build a rational second nature in which rights prevail over oppression. Irrational tradition should be overcome, but if reason is to retain its own claims, the past must not be robbed of its independent objectivity.

These agendas endow modernity with an unrivalled authority that no passage of time can diminish. Through the revolutionary act of identifying validity with rational autonomy, modernity sets its norms free of the dependence upon privileged foundations that plagues every alternative form of life. If thought and action are not autonomous, they owe their design to some independent factor, which serves as their ground. Any attempt to sanction theory or practice then falls into the dilemma of foundational justification, whose diagnosis is as elusively simple as is its cure. So long as legitimacy is sought by appeal to a privileged foundation conferring validity, what possesses validity, the foundationally sanctioned thought or conduct, is something different from the foundation that endows it with validity. This difference guarantees that the source of normativity can never satisfy its own standard for justification. With justification equated with being determined by the privileged foundation, that foundation can only enjoy the same legitimacy it confers if it is grounded upon itself. In that case, however, it would lose its constitutive character as the prior foundation of something else, a character depending upon the distinction between ground and grounded. To possess normativity, the source of normativity would instead have to become something self-grounded. The foundation and its derivative would thereby become identical, supplanting the ground/grounded dichotomy with a unity where what boasts legitimacy is determined by itself. So long, however, as what counts as legitimate is not self-determined, legitimation retains the self-debilitating distinction between founding source and founded recipient that is the fatal bane of every version of foundationalism. This distinction not only robs foundational justification of the ability to achieve coherence, but drives it to eliminate its own defining distinction once it attempts to become self-referentially consistent.

The resulting solution to the legitimation problem of foundationalism testifies to how the normativity of self-determination is not rooted in any foundation. On the contrary, the normativity of self-determination is the very outcome of foundational justification's own attempt to be consistent and overcome its own incoherence. Instead of depending upon the support of some external criterion, the legitimacy of freedom emerges from the immanent critique of foundationalism, a critique coming to fruition when the calling into question of the validity of any privileged foundation ineluctably entails canceling the distinction between legitimating foundation and the bearer of legitimacy. The freedom from foundations of self-determination thus has a double necessity: not only would self-determined thought, action, art, and religion lose their autonomy if their measure lay outside them, but the very appeal to an external standard ends up ratifying the exclusive legitimacy of freedom the moment any such standard is evaluated on its own terms.

These relations define the fundamental divide separating modernity from its opponents as well as the limitations of their opposition. If modernity be the form of civilization liberating itself from foundations by embracing the normativity of rational autonomy, it stands distinguished from pre-modern and post-modern community, the two other basic forms that civilization can have with regard to foundations.

Pre-Modernity and Legitimation

Pre-modern civilization takes its bearings by tradition, understanding legitimation to reside in a privileged foundation. Instead of placing theory and practice before the tribunal of autonomous reason, pre-modernity accepts the legitimacy of given custom, privileging the particular heritage in which it locates its roots. Although pre-modern civilization may coexist with or follow the demise of a modern community, pre-modernity is logically antecedent to modernity insofar as modernity emerges by calling tradition into question and struggling to erect institutions realizing the sovereignty of reason and freedom. Because the institutions of freedom are not rooted in any antecedent custom, nor conditioned by anything other than the general prerequisites of rational agency, these modern conventions are potentially global and, perhaps, intergalactic in application. By contrast, because pre-modernity finds legitimacy in the given practices of a particular tradition limited in space and time, it has a local, parochial reach that cannot consistently attain the global hegemony that a rootless modernity can achieve. Further, because the traditions of pre-modernity are not determined by reason and the concept of self-determination, but simply given by the contingencies of convention, pre-modern civilization can possess an inexhaustible variety, whose particulars can be known not by philosophical thought but only by historical cognition.

No matter what shape pre-modernity takes or where and when it appears, it always faces legitimation problems once the sanctity of its privileged practices is questioned. Because they are founded upon a particular tradition, whose authority resides simply in its givenness, each competing heritage has just as arbitrary a standing as any other. Since each tradition is itself a contingent convention whose claim to privilege cannot be rationally justified, nothing but the force of prevailing acceptance can uphold its authority. Once that acceptance begins to crumble under the weight of some alternative, one foundation gets supplanted by another, subject to the same contest for power.

Consequently, when pre-modern movements challenge modernity for violating their cherished traditions, the accusation has force only for those who already accept the authority of pre-modern roots. Even if the pre-modern reaction accuses a modern community of failing to achieve its promised emancipation, that failure cannot sanction pre-modern tradition if it too fails to conform to modern ideals of freedom.

The Post-Modern Challenge to Modernity and the Limits of the Enlightenment

In order for the claims of modernity to be called into question, more must be done than appeal to a privileged tradition or expose the inconsistencies of a particular modern community. Declaiming a discrepancy between modern institutions and some given way of life will not suffice since the privilege of any tradition can always be denied. Unmasking hypocrisies in some modern civilization, on the other hand, still leaves open the possibility that a more consistent modern regime could overcome those duplicities. Accordingly, if modernity is to be contested, the very possibility of fulfilling the modern project must be cast into doubt.

Post-modernity defines itself on the basis of just such suspicion. Although post-modernity recognizes the unjustifiable arbitrariness of every privileged tradition, post-modernity denies that normativity can escape the hold of foundations. Whereas modernity aspires to recognize no other authority than the autonomy of reason, conduct, artistic creativity, and religious practice, post-modernism counters that the alleged independence of rational autonomy is a sham. Like every other candidate for normativity, freedom, post-modernism declares, equally rests upon foundations, whose immediate givenness renders them subject to the same charge of arbitrariness as any alternate privileged given.

Post-modernism finds easy confirmation of this dependence in the Enlightenment's attempt to provide foundations for autonomous reason, right, and aesthetic worth. Starting with Descartes, continuing with his empiricist counterparts, and culminating in Kant and successive transcendental philosophers, Enlightenment theorists have pursued the strategy of overcoming dogmatic appeals to the putative givens of nature by turning instead to the structure of cognition as the foundation of objective knowledge. Transforming first philosophy from ontology into epistemology, these theorists supposed that the pitfalls of direct appeal to given reality could be avoided by locating conditions of knowing that determine the character of the objects of knowledge. Rather than contemplating a reality that is simply found, this modern strategy fixes upon the structure of knowing as the foundation from which objectivity is constructed. Yet, as post-modernism can duly observe, this in turn involves its own appeal to the given—in this case, the givenness of the structures of knowing by which objectivity is allegedly constructed. These epistemological givens are just as immediately contemplated as the ontological givens that pre-critical metaphysics dogmatically intuited. The basic dilemma of foundationalism applies once more: the conditions of objective knowledge cannot be known to constitute objectivity unless they themselves can be known with the same authority as the knowledge they found. But how can the conditions of knowing be objectively known if they remain antecedent epistemological foundations that must be stipulated *before* the limits of objective knowledge can be determined? The successive turns to the ego, the psychology of human understanding, the transcendental apperception, ordinary and ideal language, the hermeneutic situation, and every other candidate for privileged determiner of objectivity all run up against the same stumbling block—the knowing of the conditions of reference that is to precede objective knowledge stands in need of its own critique. Otherwise every claim about the character and privileged role of the alleged epistemological foundation remains no more than an arbitrary assertion. But how can valid claims be made about the foundations of knowing without taking for granted the adequacy of the cognition that addresses that question? The impasse seems insurmountable. Any attempt to identify foundations for reason is bound to fail.

Completely analogous difficulties plague the Enlightenment strategies to rescue right and beauty from the metaphysical assumptions of tradition. Enlightenment ethics takes its cue from the inability of pre-modern ethics to identify and legitimate a highest good, without which all ends appear relative, condemning conduct to an aimless futility. Every candidate for highest good faces the same legitimation problem as any other privileged foundation—because the highest good is that which confers value upon all other goods, it cannot derive its own value from any other factor. But then nothing but its own given content can be the source of its authority. Yet every other competitor for highest good has a given content of its own that can just as well be immediately affirmed. If no highest good can be justifiably privileged any more than can any first principle of reality, what options does ethics have left? The absence of a highest good certainly sets the will free from any prescribed end, but does this liberation redeem conduct from the aimless quandary of nihilism? The Enlightenment answer is that the collapse of the quest for a highest good provides the foundation for liberty to take its place as the exclusive locus of value in conduct, setting the stage for modernity to erect institutions of freedom, liberating the future from the past. Yet can liberty escape the pitfalls of a highest good if it confers legitimacy upon any end that is willed in accord with its privileged form of volition? Whether interpreted empirically as the freedom of desire that utilitarianism advances or conceived a priori as the formal willing of social contract construction, liberty has a given content of its own, defined in function of the self as a natural endowment that precedes all conventions. Can its given agency command exclusive legitimacy any more than any given end?

If ends can no longer be rationally ordered, then every desire and disposition stands on a par, suggesting that nothing can favor one action, character, or institution over another except a greater quantity of resulting desire satisfaction. Yet if desires are qualitatively different, contingent, and variable, and therefore devoid of any necessary harmony, a utilitarian calculus can hardly be applied, let alone dispel the nihilist challenge of why desire satisfaction should override any competing consideration. Lacking the universality that would permit the desire satisfaction of one individual to be realized compatibly with that of others, the liberty of desire simply cannot fit the form of right and occupy the position of a privileged ethical principle.

To enjoy the universal entitlement of an Archimedean right, liberty must abstract from the particularity of its empirical ends and obtain a lawful form guaranteeing the harmony of its realizations. What better meets this requirement than the agency of property relations, where individuals invest their will in an external factor that can be recognized as the receptacle of their volition because it does not intrude upon the respective domains in which others have laid their own wills? In determining oneself as an owner, what counts is not the desire satisfaction that ownership brings oneself or others, but simply the achievement of a recognized embodiment of will that stands in harmony with the analogous embodiments of other owners. Unlike pursuing one's desires, exercising one's freedom of ownership, be it by staking an original ownership claim, using one's property, or transferring it by contract, involves willing in a manner that not only automatically coexists with the ownership rights of others, but operates prior to the institution of any further forms of community. Property ownership is predicated upon the mutual recognition of a plurality of private domains, for ownership only gives persons title to use what is theirs, in distinction from the property of others. The right to property logically precedes all other exercise of rights, for no association of freedom can consist of members who lack recognition as owners of at least their own body and stand liable to appropriation by the will of another. For this reason, the right of contract can figure as a foundation for ethical construction, occupying a primordial state of nature preceding all legitimate convention from out of which institutions can gain sanction as contractually chosen instruments for upholding property right. This familiar formula for social contract theory inaugurates the liberal challenge to pre-modern tradition, setting universal property right as a revolutionary principle overturning all conventions that restrict the freedom of contract.

Yet why should the formal right of property owners reign supreme? Taken as a principle of ethical construction, property right falls into the very trap of foundationalism that waylaid the quest for a highest good and put liberty at center stage. To play the Archimedean role of foundation of justice, property right must lay claim to an antecedently given content that somehow warrants the privilege to confer validity upon whatever conventions can be derived from it. Although property right does not consist of a given end, it still presents a form of willing with just as much a given content as any highest good. Consequently, the form of its agency does not derive from the determining procedure for which it is put to constructive use. Yet if legitimacy consists in being the outcome of its choice procedure, the contracting will cannot itself enjoy the validity it alone confers. Not only does it determine derivative institutions different from itself, but these grounded conventions owe their design not to themselves but to the prior choice procedure whose own authority remains an immediate stipulation. In both respects, the Enlightenment project of procedural ethical construction remains caught in the foundational categories of positing, of positor and posited, of ground and grounded, failing to account for the self-determination with which modernity distinguishes itself from pre-modern tradition and post-modern irony. Neither the collapse of an ethics of a highest good nor the incompatibilities of the freedom of desire can sanction the formal volition of social contract and its procedural ethics. Their failings certify only their own inadequacy, leaving intact the challenge of nihilism and the abiding problem of justifying a principle of willing that founds without being founded.

The modern quest for beauty appears to suffer a similar fate, if the Enlightenment be allowed to provide the measure for modernity. Whereas pre-modern thought sought beauty in mimetic congruence with reality, Enlightenment aesthetics rejects founding beauty in natural form since mimesis either reduces beauty to a redundant copy, erasing the distinction between the prosaic and the beautiful, or condemns beauty to a deficient replica, whose deviating individuality is deprived of any aesthetic worth. Instead, Enlightenment thought turns to the process of reception to indirectly determine aesthetic worth, just as its foundational epistemology constructed objectivity from structures of knowing and its procedural ethics conjured right from social contract.

If aesthetic experience be construed in empirical terms, aesthetics can only provide standards of beauty by appealing to some common psychological nature that allows all viewers to respond with comparable pleasure to the same appearances. Yet, like empirical desire, an empirical taste for beauty cannot command the coherent universality norms demand. Appeal to human psychology either reduces aesthetic response to an instinctual necessity from which normativity disappears or to a provisionally observed pattern of response to which necessity can no more be ascribed than can juridical privilege. If alternately the empirical process of reception be defined by the cultural conventions of language or of some institutionalized "artworld" analogous problems persist. If aesthetic worth be measured by what those conventions posit as art or beauty, the question remains as to why the favored objects qualify, a question that has no answer if objective features are not the locus of aesthetic worth and the defining conventions operate without any other identifiable grounds.

Moving away from empirically given psychological or conventional factors to formal, a priori features of aesthetic experience might seem to offer the same benefits as the move from psychologism to transcendental constitution in epistemology and the move from utility to property right in liberal ethics. Aesthetic standards might now command the universality and necessity required, even if both be rooted in the subjective or intersubjective character of reception, rather than in the objective features of the object of beauty. Yet so long as beauty be founded in the determining process of reception, all objects owe their aesthetic value to the same foundation, reducing beauty to a universal property that is fundamentally indifferent to the individuality that distinguishes the originality of fine art and the creativity of artistry from the common form of artifacts and the rote technique of craft. Because Enlightenment aesthetics determines beauty by a common process of reception given independently of the individual appearances to which beauty is ascribed, all chance is lost of capturing the unity of meaning and configuration, the inseparability of sensuous detail and significance that is the counterpart of the creativity and originality in fine art. Just as autonomy is forsaken if validity derives from a choice procedure preceding the conduct it sanctions, so the individuality of beauty falls beyond grasp if the standard of taste lies in a separate ground, be it a form of reality to be imitated by every work with the same topic or a structure of reception common to every appearance judged to have aesthetic value.

Religion suffers similar dilemmas when Enlightenment thinking repudiates appeals to given objective determinations of the divine and instead turns to personal subjectivity as the determining source of faith. Just as things-in-themselves become unknowable occasions for epistemological construction, so God becomes an unapproachable, indeterminate remain for Enlightenment Deism, which reduces faith to a formal subjective attitude, devoid of any fixed content. With the divine deprived of a definite nature, religious observance and religious community have no ground for any specific forms of worship. Instead, individuals follow their own heart in acknowledging an absolute of which they can know nothing. Yet can faith retain significance if it be limited to an inchoate pietism of feeling that otherwise leaves the conduct of life unperturbed? If believers renounce all determinate knowledge of the divine, and with it, all religious dogmas and organized worship, and instead regard their faith as at most a commitment to be moral, can religion coherently claim that the essence of humanity still resides in relating to the divine? Can faith avoid withering away as a redundant, superfluous adjunct to conscience, whose own subjectivity leaves any objective good beyond reach? And can individuals justify the supremacy they accord their own heart in determining piety? Is it any less an arbitrary foundation than the dogmas about the divine against which they rebel?[1]

At each turn, in knowledge, in conduct, in beauty, and in faith, the Enlightenment project fails to escape the dilemmas of tradition by failing to overcome foundations in theory, practice, aesthetic judgment, and religion. By substituting construction for contemplation, liberty for a highest good, a critique of taste for mimetic fidelity, and an empty feeling for objective faith, Enlightenment thought still remains within the foundational orbit that undermines all its efforts to provide a viable justification for modernity.

For post-modernism, this result signifies much more than that the Enlightenment's attempt to provide foundations for autonomous reason is

---

1   For a classic statement of these criticisms of Enlightenment Deism and Pietism, see G.W.F. Hegel, *Lectures on the Philosophy of Religion: One Volume Edition, The Lectures of 1827*, ed. Peter Hodgson, trans. R.F. Brown, P.C. Hodgson, and J.M. Stewart with assistance of H.S. Harris (Berkeley: University of California Press, 1988), pp. 485–6.

a hopeless endeavor. Post-modernism further concludes that modernity's project of advancing autonomy in reason, conduct, art, and religion is equally quixotic. To come to this conclusion by exposing the dilemmas of epistemological foundationalism, procedural justice, the critique of taste, and deism only makes sense if the autonomy of reason, conduct, beauty, and religious practice cannot be justified without appeal to foundations. The failure of the Enlightenment can only serve as an indictment of modernity if post-modernism further presumes that reason, conduct, art, and religion cannot escape the hold of foundations. Rejecting the possibility of radical independence, of liberating the future from the past, post-modernism accordingly maintains that thinking, action, artistry, and worship can only take their normative bearings from privileged vocabularies that foundations provide. Because, however, post-modernism understands that the appeal to foundations can never achieve self-legitimation, post-modernism recognizes that these foundations must lack the features that justification would require. Instead of being universal, necessary, and conceptually transparent, the privileged foundations are actually particular, contingent, and opaque to reason. Consequently, whatever norms are grounded upon them are merely values, that is, relative, perspectival ideals whose claim to universality can only really represent an attempt by their particular authors to impose their will upon all others.

Thus, even though post-modernism joins pre-modernity in accepting the hegemony of foundations over human affairs, post-modernism rejects the possibility of endowing any one tradition with privileged authority. Recognizing instead that all foundations are particular and arbitrary, post-modernism can offer only one recipe for a civilization of its own: in knowing, in action, in art, and even in faith, a consistently post-modern community will advance norms that are openly particular and arbitrary. Instead of conforming to pre-modern tradition or following the universal aspirations of modernity's embrace of freedom, post-modern civilization will mold itself upon a brazen will to power, oppressing without veils or excuses. The values that post-modernity advances will give expression to the past as embodied in the given particular character of its agents. Yet because epistemological claims are made with the same perspectival arbitrariness as ethical, aesthetic, and religious values, post-modernity must treat the past as an instrument for advancing the triumph of the consistent will to power that it opposes to the alleged illusion of self-determination and its universal modern rights.

Post-modernity may well regard all foundations and their derivative values with an irony befitting their historical contingency and relativity.

Yet ironic detachment is not an invitation to multicultural toleration or democracy, as irresolute post-modernists would like to believe.[2] Acknowledgment of the arbitrariness of all values provides no rationale for toleration, for toleration is itself a particular ideal to which irony should be indifferent. If anything, an active opposition prevails, for toleration and democracy rest upon a very firm commitment to the equal right of each culture and political agent, a commitment that can only be realized through the internal reformation or external curbing of incompatible, intolerant value systems. To find consistent expression, post-modern irony would better pursue a frankly perspectival world order, where the arbitrary will of a single unconstrained leader imposes its domination for the few with whom it shares some given particular identity.

The Dilemma behind the Rhetoric of Post-Modernism

So long as modernity finds no better defenders than the foundational thinkers of the Enlightenment, post-modernism can readily achieve a rhetorical triumph, identifying the legitimation of modernity with the Enlightenment project, unmasking the foundational dilemmas of the latter, and deconstructing the will to power allegedly underlying and subverting the universalist claims of modern civilization. Yet even in this endeavor, post-modernism cannot free itself of the very duplicities it condemns. To supersede pre-modernity and modernity alike, post-modernity must deny the autonomy of reason, conduct, art, and religion, and uphold the hegemony of historically contingent foundations over all the value-positing activities distinguishing humanity. If, however, post-modernism's diagnosis of the conditioned character of theory and practice is true, how can it conform to its own verdict? If all knowing and doing is conditioned by unjustifiable conventions, how can post-modernism be more than a perspectival ideology whose claims are themselves relative to its own contingent foundations? In order to legitimate its global judgment upon discourse and conduct against competing views, post-modernism must transcend the hegemony of contingent foundations, contradicting its own thesis. If post-modernism instead admits to being one ideology among others, it can hardly present its characterization of modernity as more than a strategic tool of its own self-assertion. Even if

---

2   For a prime example of this self-delusion of irresolute post-modernism, see Richard Rorty, *Contingency, Irony, and Solidarity* (Cambridge, UK: Cambridge University Press, 1989).

the Enlightenment project collapses when subjected to self-critique, post-modernism cannot justifiably maintain that modernity is to be measured by the Enlightenment and that autonomous reason cannot be given an internally consistent account and a coherent realization.

Modernity beyond Enlightenment and Post-Modernism

What post-modernism never even considers is the key to modernity's break with tradition, a key that the Enlightenment equally ignores. This is the revolutionary insight that self-determination does not and can not have foundations. Unless freedom's independence from foundations can be comprehended, the normativity of truth, right, beauty, and religious faith cannot be redeemed from the dogmas that have cast them under a cloud of suspicion. Neither pre-modern tradition, nor Enlightenment thought, nor post-modernism can absorb this crucial comprehension so long as they retain their common belief that the logic of justification is identical to the logic of foundationalism. Each strikes a different attitude to the identity they all acknowledge, pre-modernists trusting the authority of a particular foundation, Enlightenment thinkers advancing foundations that are privileged determiners rather than privileged givens, and post-modernists acquiescing to the ubiquity of foundations while acknowledging the historical contingency of each one. Amidst this diversity, none dares wager that justification could avoid appeal to some foundation or other.

Far easier is recognizing that justification is always hobbled so long as it rests upon some antecedent ground, conferring validity upon something other than itself. What could be more absurd than looking for the basis of truth in something outside the truth, in searching for right in what is not right itself, in locating beauty in what itself lacks all aesthetic worth, or grounding faith in something beyond belief? Certainly any recourse to foundations warrants skeptical detachment, but is post-modern irony any less naive in its acceptance of the hegemony of foundational justification? An anti-foundationalism that decries truth, right, beauty, and faith by unmasking the contingency of all privileged paradigms is an anti-foundationalism in name only. Not only does such an impostor offer its own grand narrative of the global conditioning of reason, conduct, artistry, and religion by historical conventions, but it lacks the candor to admit the incoherence of its own unconditioned claims about theory and practice.

The authentic alternative to foundations is so close at hand in the dilemmas of foundationalism, so radical in its break with tradition, so potent in paralyzing the ideological challenge of fascism, and so pervasive in a modern age that the simplicity of its solution risks making it virtually invisible. A civilization emerging from oppressive tradition, weaned on the Enlightenment misconception of modernity, and tempted by post-modern irony is thoroughly accustomed to see no justification if foundations are not advanced. What appears without ground is assumed to be arbitrary, a posit of a will that conceals its founding authorship. A truly groundless content is simply beyond comprehension for a viewpoint blind to validity without foundations. Yet, seeing what foundational thinking finds invisible is precisely the challenge on which the justification of modernity hangs.

Self-determination is inconceivable in foundational terms. To qualify as self-determined, something must be what it has determined itself to be. The character of self-determination cannot be something immediately given, for any given content would not have resulted from self-determination, but would be an endowment deriving from some other source. Whatever content self-determination possesses must instead arise in the process by which the self-determined self engenders itself as free. Accordingly, freedom cannot have any grounds, but must rather ground itself in the process constitutive of self-determination.

The relation between normativity and self-determination resides in this independence from external grounding that has its positive expression in the self-grounding character of freedom. The internal logic of foundational argument already prepares the way for this connection without need of appeal to any competing truths. If a foundation confers validity, the foundation cannot possess the validity it provides unless it rests upon itself just as does what it founds. The foundation lacks validity unless it becomes self-grounding, transforming itself from a foundation both different and antecedent to what it founds into a subject that determines itself. Applied to the four domains of normativity, the outcome of foundationalism signals that truth must rest upon itself, that right must be defined by nothing but right, and that beauty and religion must be autonomous.

These injunctions lose their tautological appearance the moment autonomy in reason, conduct, art, and religion get developed in theory or confirmed as keystones of modern practice.

Chapter 2

Modernity and Secular Culture

Modernity and Philosophy

Modernity can no more do without autonomous reason than reason can do without autonomy. Pre-modern philosophy was content to seek the principle of reality without worrying about what came first in thinking. Water, atoms, being, becoming, spirit, substance, the divine, to name just a few favored options, were advanced in turn as ultimate foundations of what is. Yet, since each candidate for first principle of ontology had to have a non-derivative content, resting on nothing else and being that on which all else rests, nothing could certify the supremacy of one alternative over another. Any attempt to offer a ground to justify some candidate for first principle of reality only subverts the primacy of that candidate, while introducing a ground just as subject to question. In light of this dilemma, Enlightenment thought turned its attention to what came first in thinking, as if locating some privileged ground in the process of knowing could overcome ontological relativity. Either strategy puts philosophy in the same bind: the moment philosophy begins with a foundation, the character and primacy of the privileged term cannot help but be taken for granted as something decided before and, therefore, outside of philosophical investigation. Philosophical reason thereby condemns itself to heteronomy, that is, to determination by something else. Instead of accounting for all its own terms, philosophy allows itself to be ruled by contents it has not justified, undermining any hope of reason legitimating itself and serving as the ultimate tribunal for modernity's break with the past. If philosophy is not to take its own method and subject matter for granted, but treat its form and content as philosophical problems to be decided within philosophy, reason must operate without any preconceptions concerning what it should be addressing or how it should proceed. Yet in that case, philosophy must begin without any initial claims about reality or knowing, that is, without any determinate foundations. To do so, philosophy proper must begin without any determinate method or content, and if philosophy is to move beyond being an empty word to arrive at any determinate claims in any determinate order, both the content and its form of presentation must develop without reliance upon any external factors. Philosophical thought must therefore be self-determining, giving itself a content through its own efforts whose form must equally be the product of philosophical reason. To escape dogmatism, philosophy must overcome foundations by developing as an autonomous reason. Moreover, because philosophy cannot begin with the assumption of any determinate ground, the self-determination that philosophical reason must realize can be nothing but self-determination per se, rather than the autonomous development of some given substrate. The form of philosophical truth turns out to be identical with the logic of self-determination.

This revolutionary outcome might appear hopelessly at odds with common understandings of logic, given how traditional and Enlightenment thought have treated logic as a formal deductive discipline, whose rules of inference are axiomatic givens applying not to themselves but to extraneously given subject matters. Yet, the very project of logic cannot possibly meet success unless it converges with the same identification of validity and autonomy that emerges from philosophy's grappling with foundations. As a thinking of thinking, logic begins with a unity of method and content, where knowing and its object are indistinguishable. If logic is to prescribe what valid thinking is, the thinking that logic employs must be identical with valid thinking itself. Logic would, however, be begging its question if it started out with either a determinate method or a determinate content. If logic is to establish the form and content of valid thinking, these must both be the result, rather than the presupposed starting point of its labors. Whatever is established within logic must then develop itself, for nothing outside of logical investigation can legitimately furnish any material or procedure. Since logic must begin without any givens, the autonomous subject matter it ends up presenting can be nothing other than self-determination, once more confirming how the legitimacy of reason depends upon supplanting reliance upon foundations with foundation-free autonomy.

Precisely *how* logic thinks valid thinking and *how* philosophy presents the autonomous development of self-determination are matters that lie beyond the identification of normativity and freedom. Although these questions have received little attention outside of Hegel's much maligned *Science of Logic*,[1] whether any modern thinker has yet satisfactorily answered them has no bearing upon the possibility of doing so or upon

---

1   For an investigation into the tie between freedom, normativity, and conceptual determination, see Richard Dien Winfield, *From Concept to Objectivity: Thinking Through Hegel's Subjective Logic* (Aldershot, UK: Ashgate, 2006).

the possibility of legitimating modernity. What can be said without reserve is that if philosophy remains caught within the foundationalisms of traditional ontology or Enlightenment epistemology, reason can never achieve the radical self-responsibility and self-legitimation of a genuinely autonomous thinking. But if philosophy overcomes foundations by thinking autonomously, modernity can possess the self-legitimating reason it needs to break with tradition, disarm the post-modern challenge, and liberate the future of thought from the past while rescuing the past from the ideological designs for tomorrow.

The realization of modernity does not, however, depend upon the completion of the philosophical defense of modernity. Modern institutions of freedom can be founded and sustained so long as individuals interact with sufficient rectitude to uphold the rights constitutive of a civilization at home with self-determination. How many individuals act in accord with modern conventions while holding a philosophical theory legitimating those institutions is something left open by their mere compliance. This is reflected by how the ideological defense of modernity has so often been waged with inappropriate resources deriving from Enlightenment thought. Although this leaves the defenders of modernity poorly armed to refute critiques from post-modernists and anti-modern fundamentalists alike, it does not mean that the appeal of emancipation will be unpersuasive.

In any event, so long as modern institutions prevail, the intellectual climate will at least be shielded from the inquisitions that use public power to impede calling into question traditional foundations, both secular and sacred. In that respect, at least, the struggle for modernity will facilitate its philosophical defense, which may well make that struggle all the more successful.

Modernity and the Institutions of Right

What modernity entails for theory, holds all the more palpably for practice. Just as truth must ground itself, so what is right must break with foundations and give itself its own order. Unless conduct is self-determined, unless institutions comprise the reality of freedom, the normativity of practice will lie in external factors whose own legitimacy remains always in question. Yet how can conduct escape the hold of historical conditions and achieve self-determination? Is modernity's whole project to overthrow traditional oppression with universal institutions of freedom an illusory dream?

Enlightenment ethics already raised the banner of liberty as the only viable alternative to the traditional pursuit of a highest good through virtue and character. Yet because Enlightenment ethics treated liberty as a foundation for ethical construction, be it by employing a utilitarian calculus or social contract, self-determination got conflated with the structure of positing, where what determines is different from what gets determined.[2] This reduction precludes any possibility of coherently conceiving freedom, for so long as the will is thought to have a given nature preceding its volition, it can never exhibit the reflexivity of autonomy, where what determines and what gets determined are one and the same. Self-determination easily appears to be an utter impossibility—first, because no willing can take place without a "natural" agency endowed with a capacity of choice preceding each and every act of will, and secondly, because no will can determine its own character by itself without falling into the paradox of having to act upon itself with an agency that is supposed to issue from its own activity. Because of just this difficulty of conceiving agent and patient as one and the same, Plato early on abandoned all thought of self-determination, concluding instead that the soul must be divided into a ruling, rather than self-ruling, component, lording over a subject accessory, just as the polis would have to be divided into a guardian class ruling over a subject class.[3]

What resolves these difficulties is emancipating the conception of freedom from the parameter of the single subject, a parameter that locked Enlightenment thought into conflating self-determination with positing, the determining of something by an antecedently given determiner. If freedom is conceived not as a function of the self but as a conventional structure of right in which a plurality of agents interact in function of universal entitlements, the reflexivity of self-determination becomes a possibility not so unfamiliar for a modern age.

To be self-determined, an agent must determine not only what ends are willed, but who does the willing. Instead of being merely a natural endowment preceding volition, the agency of self-determined conduct must have a character that is determined by its own willing. Autonomous agency must thus be artificial or conventional, rather than natural.

---

2   This is exhibited in the tendency of Enlightenment philosophers to think of the free will in terms of the categories of cause and effect, as if freedom could be made sense of as an "uncaused cause." Cause and effect categories always distinguish between what acts and what is acted upon, whereas self-determination is self-acting. The categories of freedom are not those of positing, where the determined and the determining are distinct factors.

3   Plato makes this fateful theoretical move in the *Republic*, Book IV, 430e–31a.

Although an isolated agent can never act without presupposing, rather than determining, its own given agency, the will becomes able to determine its own agency by participating in an enacted context of rights.

Self-government, the most sovereign such context, shows perhaps most clearly how self-determination involves a conventional agency that only the interaction of rights can provide. To exercise political self-determination, no natural endowments or functions of the self suffice. Although one cannot engage in self-government unless one possesses the natural, psychological, and linguistic capabilities making possible independent action and respect for the rights of others, political self-determination is impossible unless one belongs as a recognized citizen to an existing state containing the institutions of self-government. For any individual to enjoy this membership, the other citizens must simultaneously exercise their political self-determination simply because the reality of self-government consists in nothing but the political activities of self-governing citizens. Moreover, each citizen must enjoy equal political opportunity, for unless the right to political self-determination is universal, the politically privileged will lord over the rest, transforming self-government into a regime where a ruling elite imposes order upon a subject class. Because the enabling institutional context of political freedom is itself determined by the exercise of self-government, political self-determination is able to do what the individual will can never independently achieve: namely, determine not only the content of its volition but the nature of its agency. By performing their political roles, which collectively reproduce the body politic, citizens determine their own artificial, conventional agency as self-governing individuals and they do so by exercising a political right whose guaranteed exercise is part and parcel of the reality of self-government. Consequently, political freedom has normativity built into it. Self-government, like every other mode of self-determination, is itself a structure of right in which individuals impose upon themselves an entitled agency, whose conventional autonomy cannot be exercised apart from mutual recognition of its validity. Whereas Enlightenment ethics treated freedom as a principle from which valid institutions are derived, the interaction of self-determination renders freedom the reality rather than a foundation of justice.

The resulting identity between self-determination and normativity in conduct might seem vain first, if a plurality of rights calls for restraining self-determination in any of its institutional modes and, second, if the existence of the institutions of freedom is conditioned by natural, psychological, and historical factors.

The first question bears directly upon the legitimacy of political freedom, for if there be non-political rights, self-government must be prevented from overriding those entitlements, a task that seems to call for a restraining power undermining political sovereignty, as well as the exclusive validity of self-determination. The problem disappears, however, as soon as one recognizes that political freedom cannot be exercised unless non-political freedoms are simultaneously realized. In the first place, individuals can hardly claim political freedom, let alone any other right, unless they all have determined themselves as owners, enjoying recognition as proprietors of at least their own bodies, without which they remain subject to enslavement. Similarly, unless agents possess the right of moral accountability, holding one another responsible only for what they have done on purpose and only for those ramifications of their actions that are prefigured in their motives, they cannot enjoy the independent political responsibility on which self-government depends. By the same token, unless the family is transformed into an institution of freedom, where spouses codetermine household affairs independently of any other kin domination, subordinate family members can hardly enjoy equal access to society and state and participate in politics on a par with others. And without the realization of social freedom through a civil society enabling individuals to choose their occupation and needs in the market under equal protection of civil law and public welfare guarantees of equal economic opportunity, the barriers of social privilege, and the fixity of tradition will block political opportunity for the socially oppressed. Self-government therefore need not be subject to the anomaly of a higher authority to uphold pre-political right. A higher foundation is precluded, for unless the rights of property, moral, family, and social freedom are all enforced, political self-determination cannot itself exist. Hence, far from comprising a restriction upon political freedom, the non-political freedoms are necessary conditions of its own realization. Not only does self-rule require the establishment of property rights and moral, household, and social autonomy, but political freedom cannot sustain itself unless all these non-political freedoms are upheld by the state in conformity with the practice of self-government. The reality of freedom therefore comprises a self-sustaining system of rights, grounding itself through the sovereign autonomy of self-governing citizens, whose own political self-determination must uphold the totality of their freedom in order to subsist.

Admittedly, the institutions of freedom cannot maintain themselves unless a whole variety of natural, psychological, and historical conditions are at hand. The physical, chemical, and biological requirements of rational agency must be present, just as must the cultural developments that permit individuals to interact in recognition of their rights. Yet these *enabling* conditions cannot play the role of *juridical* conditions, as foundationalists would like to believe. Precisely because the physical, psychological, and linguistic conditions of rational agency underlie each and every form of convention, they can hardly provide a basis for distinguishing between the just and unjust institutions, let alone the true and false theories, that they equally make possible. For this reason, the contingency of the enabling conditions of free conduct in no way limits the normative independence of self-determination. The practical project of modernity may be frustrated in a particular time and place by natural conditions beyond rational control, such as climatic calamities, asteroid collisions, or solar burnout. Further, contingent cultural developments can always prevent freedom from prevailing over oppression. Nevertheless, wherever and whenever physical nature is permitting, the mere presence of a tradition signals the possibility of struggling for emancipation.

This struggle is not without its complications, given how the genesis of a modern civilization is determined by the very structure of the institutions of freedom. Although those institutions are defined independently of all foundations, and therefore independently of all local tradition, they need not and, indeed, cannot come into being with a reach fitting their inherent universality. The founding of the institutions of self-government is not an exercise of political freedom, or a merely political deed, for it equally involves the whole series of historical developments by which universal property right becomes recognized, moral autonomy triumphs over sacred and secular tutelage, household hierarchy is overthrown, and social bondage is overcome. Since these transformations are subject to all the contingencies of history, the first modern community cannot help but emerge in a particular time and place, bearing the contingent stamp of its regional baptism. Even though modernity may command universal validity because its institutions of freedom are independent of each and every heritage, the local character of the genesis of modernity creates a situation where a first modern civilization arises in face of pre-modern communities that have not as yet modernized themselves. The transformation of these abiding traditional communities into modern nations may then take the form of a regional assimilation, which may or may not involve direct political domination. To take our planetary experience as an example, if modernity has truly first arisen in the West, then modernization will appear as Westernization, especially if the first modern civilization still bears the mark of contingent cultural features that are incidental to the institutions of freedom. Whatever the resulting scenario, the normativity of freedom sets the standard for what should be done. Pre-modern tradition as well as post-modern tyranny ought to give way to the institutionalization of freedom, which by its very nature cannot come to fruition without the voluntary involvement of those who are to be emancipated. Consequently, the modernization following upon the emergence of the first modern nation has no other legitimate destination than the universal political independence that eliminates all trace of colonial and neo-colonial domination.

Because every institution of right involves interactions wherein individuals act in recognition of their equal opportunities, it is a fundamental mistake to identify modernity in terms of technique, where a single agency dominates objects by imposing form upon them. This mistake underlies all those characterizations of modernity as the dystopic triumph of instrumental reason, of technology, of an industrialization understood as a unilateral mastery of production and nature, of a subjection of all relations of life to an externally administered regulation. These characterizations completely ignore the non-monological, non-technical, intersubjective character of every one of the institutions of freedom to which modern emancipation is committed. Property right, moral conduct, the emancipated household, civil society, and self-government all involve correlated activities of mutual recognition, where individuals exercise rights in function of respecting the equal rights of others. In none of these spheres of modern interaction are the relations of freedom reducible to the monological manipulation of technical activity, of making. The reduction of modernity to a regime of technical manipulation, classically perpetrated by Heidegger in his essay, "The Question Concerning Technology,"[4] has since been taken up by Hannah Arendt and Michael Oakeshott in their construals of modern society as a realm of instrumental action,[5] by Horkheimer and Adorno in their global analysis of the *Dialectic of the Enlightenment*,[6] by Foucault in his deconstruction

---

4   See Martin Heidegger, *Basic Writings*, ed. David Farrell Krell (New York: Harper Collins, 1993), pp. 311–41.

5   See Hannah Arendt, *The Human Condition* (Chicago: The University of Chicago Press, 1958), and Michael Oakeshott, *On Human Conduct* (Oxford: Oxford University Press, 1975).

6   See Max Horkheimer and Theodor W. Adorno, *Dialectic of the Enlightenment: Philosophical Fragments*, trans. Edmund Jephcott (Stanford, CA: Stanford University Press, 1992).

of modern penal institutions as paradigmatic of the regimentation of modernity,[7] and most recently by Samuel Huntington in his misleading distinguishing of modernization from Westernization.[8]

Huntington, like many contemporary social scientists, identifies modernity with industrialization and technological development, while tying many of the central features of the modern institutions of freedom to the particular nature of the West. This leads him to consider modernization something that can be embraced by the most anti-Western, illiberal regimes, while regarding the institutions of freedom to be peculiarities of the Western tradition, incapable of global realization.

The industrial instrumental organizations of production and, more generally, technological progress do indeed have a necessary place within civil society, that is, the emancipated society of modernity. This is because economic freedom operates through publicly regulated commodity relations in which competition makes continual innovation in manufacturing and product design a matter of economic survival. Nonetheless, technology can operate independently of the institutions of right specific to modernity, which is why anti-modern fundamentalists can more than happily employ the most developed communications, cybernetic, and weapons technologies for their Jihad.

Whereas technology is independent of modernity, so the institutions of freedom have an inherent universality owing to their independence from external determination. Consequently, even if the West may have first experienced the rise of such institutions, they are by their very nature realizable apart from what is *peculiar* to Western civilization. Huntington may be confused about what defines modernization and Westernization, but he does recognize correctly that whereas other civilizations may resist modernization, they need not become Western to become modern. This relation applies equally to modern philosophy, modern art, and modern religion, all of which may have been pioneered in the West, but can experience and are experiencing an autonomous development elsewhere.

---

7   See Michel Foucault, *Discipline and Punish: The Birth of the Prison*, trans. Alan Sheridan (New York: Vintage Books: 1979).

8   Huntington, Samuel P., *The Clash of Civilizations and the Remaking of World Order* (New York: Simon and Schuster Paperbacks, 2003), pp. 68–72.

Modernity and Fine Art

Although modern recognition of the normativity of freedom does not preclude controversy from raging over how autonomous thought actually determines itself and what specific content defines the different institutions of freedom, the situation of fine art in modernity raises questions of a different sort. Aesthetics has always confronted the problem of how beauty can persist untarnished through the ages whereas past achievements in theory and practice lose their luster when judged by the modern standard of autonomous reason. In some respects the artistic achievements of former times seem to present no longer attainable heights and the whole place of beauty in modern culture seems to betray a diminished stature compared to past ages where right and truth had no precedence over the beautiful.

Resolving the post-modern challenge to aesthetic worth leaves an outcome of ambiguous meaning for art in modernity. The inability of either mimetic theory or the Enlightenment critique of taste to capture the individuality of beauty and comprehend the originality and creativity of fine art can be overcome by casting aside external foundations and locating the focal point of beauty in the unity of meaning and sensuous form.[9] This unity allows the individual detail of an aesthetic appearance to retain essential significance, while placing the normativity of beauty in the self-sufficient and original achievement by which a work presents a meaning worthy of universal attention in a sensuous (as in visual art or music) or imagined (as in literature) configuration uniquely suited to that significance. Unless an object of beauty can convey something of universal significance, it forfeits the breadth of appeal that allows aesthetic worth to be appreciated in any age and culture. And unless the object of beauty conveys something universally significant in a uniquely adequate shape, it sacrifices its standing as something that deserves individual attention. The normativity of freedom provides the very possibility of universally significant meanings by redeeming the search for truth, be it sacred or profane, the struggle for right, and art's own quest for beauty as affairs of fundamental meaning to which no rational agent can be irrevocably indifferent. Consequently, the meanings fit for beauty will enable art to provide an essential self-understanding

---

9   For a detailed investigation of how the internal difficulties of the mimetic and Enlightenment conceptions of beauty lead to conception focusing upon the individual unity of meaning and form, see Richard Dien Winfield, *Systematic Aesthetics* (Gainesville, FL: University Press of Florida, 1995).

for humanity, so long as the meanings in question are susceptible to sensuous or imaginative configuration. Because philosophical argument is purely conceptual, whereas secular and sacred conduct has a sensuous, imaginable dimension, it can be no accident that fine art has preeminently grappled with configuring the essential problems of religion and ethics.[10] Since, however, pre-modern, modern, and post-modern civilizations view the normativity of these configurable domains in different ways, their aesthetic options differ.[11]

Beauty might seem most amenable to pre-modern realization since pre-modern civilization finds legitimacy in the contingent existence of given tradition, which can only be captured by non-conceptual representation. Insofar as traditional values cannot be conceptually comprehended, artistic presentation would provide a better vehicle for pre-modern self-understanding than philosophical theory. Moreover, since the fundamental meanings to be expressed in traditional art cannot be properly communicated by thought alone, the images of art would seem especially suited to fit what pre-modern civilization finds fundamentally important. Not only would beauty here have special cultural significance as a privileged revelation of ultimate values, but the aesthetic unity of meaning and configuration would be achievable to supreme degree.

By contrast, modernity presents fine art with a more formidable challenge. Although subscribers to the modern spirit can look backwards in appreciation of how traditional art delivers supremely apt expressions of pre-modern self-understanding, traditional aesthetic forms can no longer give adequate artistic configuration to the revolutionary values of rational autonomy. Once validity gets identified with self-determination no given sensuous configuration can sufficiently convey what is of ultimate significance. Whereas traditional norms can be better captured by exemplary individuals than by abstract principle, the unconditioned universality of freedom is more suitably expressed by conceptual thought than by the image of any example.[12]

---

10 For a more detailed consideration of why this is so, see Winfield, *Systematic Aesthetics*, p. 112 ff.

11 For a more developed consideration of these options, see Richard Dien Winfield, *Stylistics: Rethinking the Art Forms After Hegel* (Albany, NY: State University of New York Press, 1996).

12 For further examination of these issues, see Winfield, *Stylistics*, Chapter IV, pp. 73–98.

Art that passes itself off as post-modern by making ironic use of traditional aesthetic forms is really following but one of the modernist strategies that artists may employ in giving aesthetic expression to the modern self-understanding. Whereas post-modernism forsakes freedom for the will to power in sober homage to the hegemony of foundations, "post-modern" art playfully recycles pre-modern styles and genres, quoting past examples of beauty with subjective license as if to show that no given configuration is adequate to the free creativity that rules supreme. Post-modern architecture, perhaps the most renowned exponent of this gambit, might appear polemically at complete odds with the pure abstractions of modernist "international style" construction. Nonetheless, the post-modern architectural quotation of tradition manifests the same withdrawal of authority from past canons as the modernist invention of expressly non-natural and non-traditional purities of design. The purely artificial system of serial music that brings constructed order to the arbitrary solitude of expressionist atonality is connected by the same unity of spirit with the expressly non-traditional recycling of primitive rhythms and folk melodies by early Stravinsky, Bartók, and the minimalists, as well as with the neo-classical recasting of classical forms in departure from traditional harmonic development. In each case, composers seek a musical expression for a creative autonomy that no given form can preeminently satisfy.[13] Similarly, whether modern painting opts for pre-modern delineation and coloration with expressionist abandon, the mechanical naturalism of photo-realism, the free associations of dada and surrealism, completely non-objective abstraction, or conceptual art's self-annulling retreat from image to self-reflection, the same aesthetic modernism is at work seeking to exhibit how no sensuous given can have any privileged rule over the autonomy that alone should count. The liberation from the past could not be sharper. Epic literature could provide a ready vehicle for a closed world of tradition, where individual striving has significance only within the completed frame of a national saga, where everything that appears is essential, and nothing merely inward is more than personal eccentricity or madness. The modern self-understanding needs a novel form, one in which the self-determination of the individual sets the course of development, where the yearnings of inner life demand

---

13 Contra Adorno, modern music is not just illuminating "the meaningless world," but sounding the affirmation of free subjectivity. See Theodor W. Adorno, *Philosophy of Modern Music*, trans. Anne G. Mitchell and Wesley V. Blomster (New York: Continuum, 1994), p. 133.

satisfaction over and against the contingencies of an indifferent outer world, where classical idealizations get replaced by encounters with any situation high or low and any character regal or depraved that an open future can bring.[14]

Modernity may not condemn art to death, but it has raised an aesthetic dilemma with no easy solutions. Because modern art must show how no given configurations can accord sufficient shape to autonomy, modern art risks displaying an ultimate indifference to the form and content of its images. Since aesthetic worth resides in the congruence between the configuration and fundamental meaning in the work of art, such indifference threatens to undermine the stature of modern art's own creations. For this reason, irony can be an emblem of modern art even if the conceptual adequacy of autonomous reason and autonomous conduct shields truth and right from post-modern irony.

Despite this disparity in the modern predicament of beauty on the one hand, and of truth and right on the other, the consequences for past and future remain the same. Just as the autonomies of reason and conduct make modern thought and practice a constitutively global imperative, transcending the limits of any regional heritage, so the challenge facing modern art is the summons of a universal culture, whose aesthetic productions must configure a freedom of spirit that no tradition can confine. A nostalgic multiculturalism may reanimate a museum of folklore and rote tradition, while a post-modern tyranny may banish or mummify the exceptions to its own artistic purities. A modern art, by contrast, is a genuine world art, no matter what particular languages and iconographies it employs.

---

14 For an elaboration of these contrasts between the epic and the novel, see Georg Lukács, *The Theory of the Novel*, trans. Anna Bostock (Cambridge, MA: MIT Press, 1971).

Chapter 3

Modernity and Religion

The antagonism of the war on terrorism revolves around a general tension, as pivotal for the original rise of modernity as for the ensuing modernization of post-colonial nations. This tension resides in the challenge that religion presents to modernity. The very possibility of any opposition might appear illusory insofar as modernity's institutions of freedom seem to ensure maximum cultural liberty, granting religion just as complete autonomy as art and philosophy. The universal rights of property ownership, moral accountability, marital and parental autonomy and equality, economic and legal freedom, and self-government all give individuals equal opportunities in express indifference to religious affiliation. Unlike pre-modern regimes that undercut household, social, political, and general cultural autonomy by privileging a particular faith centering some traditional heritage, modern civilization establishes religious freedom precisely by liberating the different spheres of right from any privileged religious tutelage.[1]

So long as any religion rules over a form of association, members of other faiths cannot enjoy equal opportunity. Whatever latitude subservient religions may be granted is still always subject to the whim of the dominant faith, whose advantaged position they can never share. Further, even if religious unanimity prevails, the subordination of practice to religious control subverts self-determination by subjecting individuals to a rule of life dictated by a religious dogma to which they must submit. Consequently, although all may adhere to the same faith, none retain the entitlement to choose their faith independently and enjoy prerogatives indifferent to religious affiliation at home, in society, in politics, or in the court of conscience.

---

1   For this reason, it is wrong to claim, without qualification, as Huntington does, that "religion … is the principal defining characteristic of civilizations" (Samuel P. Huntington, *The Clash of Civilizations and the Remaking of World Order* (New York: Simon and Schuster Paperbacks, 2003), p. 253). This may be true of most pre-modern civilizations, but the secularization of modernity frees every institution of freedom from identification by religion.

Modernity, by contrast, makes religious toleration possible by rendering religion a private matter, enabling family, social, and political life to become independent secular domains whose emancipation from clerical domination first provides the space for self-determination to be realized. It might thus appear that modernity's privatization of religious practice overcomes any possible conflict between religion and secular institutions, allowing total toleration of religious diversity. Is this not what de Tocqueville could celebrate, in observing how the most modern nation of his day, the young United States, could combine the most fervently and diversely religious citizenry with radical separation of church and state?[2]

The religious freedom that modernity makes possible, however, can only apply to religions that are compatible with toleration of both other faiths and spheres of right emancipated from direct religious rule. If religion automatically fit these requirements, universal religious toleration would be unproblematic and any opposition between modernity and faith would be precluded.

Yet can all religions be tolerated? Can they all be privatized? Indeed, can any religion remain true to the basic aspirations of faith if it accepts the limitations required for a creed to accommodate religious freedom and the correlative independent secular domains of modernity?

The Generic Nature of Religion

Religion generically represents the truth of humanity in divinity, such that individuals must relate to the divine to attain their true essence.

Religion hereby involves representation insofar as it takes the divine to be both transcendent and in essential relation to humanity. The divine is transcendent insofar as it is greater than everything finite and contingent, without which religion could claim no serious importance. Yet religion must also take the divine to be essentially related to humanity since otherwise the divine would have no bearing upon human existence, being neither something of which one can be conscious nor something to which one can, let alone need direct one's conduct. These features render religion representational because representation always presents its content both as given independently of the awareness that represents it and as revealed

---

2   See Alexis de Tocqueville, *De La Démocratie En Amérique* (Paris: Garnier-Flammarion, 1981), I, p. 401 ff.

within that awareness.³ In the case of religious representation, the content is not just something existing on its own, but the absolute, offering humanity the possibility of surmounting everything relative and transient, and partaking in what is of unconditioned value.

By turning to what is absolute, religion shares with art and philosophy a concern for truth without qualification. Unlike ideology, which presents a persuasive case to achieve predetermined ends, religion, like art and philosophy, addresses the most fundamental truth, without which no ends can be known to be choiceworthy.⁴ This common concern with unconditioned truth, however, takes an essentially different form in each case. Art addresses truth as beauty, creating intuitable or imagined works whose unity of meaning and configuration presents what is of fundamental significance to humanity in the exemplary individuality of artistic creations. Philosophy thinks truth, grasping objectivity in its conceptual determination, leaving behind the individual shapes of art, and relying exclusively upon the universality of thought. By contrast, religion has faith in the absolute, believing in the divine. This belief may support its credo with works of sacred art and philosophical justifications of religious dogma, but belief itself remains distinct from the imagining of beauty and the conceptualization of truth. What distinguishes belief from the appreciation of works of art and thinking the truth is not the content of belief, which may well converge with the meaning of art and philosophical speculation. Rather, what sets religion apart is the form of faith, the element of belief that contains something very different from the disinterested intuition of beauty and the abstraction of reason. This element is feeling, which gives faith a piety lacking in aesthetic reception and philosophical cognition.

---

3   The fundamental role of representation in religion is duly emphasized by Hegel in his *Lectures on the Philosophy of Religion*. For a revealing discussion of Hegel's treatment of this point, see Emil Fackenheim, *The Religious Dimension in Hegel's Thought* (Boston: Beacon Press, 1967), pp. 53–4, 122, and Louis Dupré, *A Dubious Heritage: Studies in the Philosophy of Religion after Kant* (New York: Paulist Press, 1977), Chapter 3 "Hegel's Religion as Representation," pp. 53–72.

4   This is why it is a mistake to treat religion as just ideology, or, for that matter, to follow Marx, Nietzsche, and much contemporary social science in regarding ideology and religion as equivalent in function. Nonetheless, religion can be used for ideological purposes, especially when it gets enlisted in domestic politics or to motivate war. For a discussion of these issues, see Hannah Arendt, *Essays in Understanding 1930–1954*, ed. Jerome Kohn (New York: Harcourt Brace & Company, 1994), pp. 374–5, 377, 384.

Like all feeling, piety involves an inward state in which the psyche communes with its own modifications. As such, feeling has a singularity, reflecting how it is enclosed within an individual self and how it takes a wordless, emotive form lacking the inherent communicability of thought, whose universal determinations need language for their formulation. Although feeling is singular, piety does not remain enclosed within the subjectivity of the believer. Piety has an object and that object cannot be an ineffable unknown if believers are to have something in which to have faith. The object of piety has a very specific content, generic to all religion, for piety is a feeling about what is most universal and unconditioned—the divine. Anything less will not do as a worthy object of worship. Moreover, piety is a feeling for the absolute to which the pious individual must relate in order to achieve what is of fundamental importance in life. If religion involved just a conception of the divine, devoid of any feeling, the divine would be entertained in detachment from one's singular concreteness. As felt, however, the representation of the divine occurs essentially in the individuals' own personal being, laying hold of the heart in all its singularity. Through piety, the divine becomes *my* God, rather than an anonymous idea to which I stand indifferent. Only through the involvement of sentiment does religion entail any devotion.[5]

Because feeling, unlike reason, cannot operate just with abstractions, religion must represent the divine in a non-conceptual form, utilizing images and narratives to portray the truth about the transcendent absolute and how individuals are to relate to it to achieve their true essence, that is, to achieve salvation. Religious sentiment relates to the divine through the mediation of these representations.

Piety, however, is not just a matter of having feelings in response to images and narratives about the divine. Because religion enjoins individuals to not just become aware of the divine, but seek their true essence by relating to the absolute, piety must join with activity.

This activity involves in the first instance worship, where individuals express their piety in specific practices. These may be performed individually, without reference to others. However, the divine is not of fundamental importance for just a single individual. Religious representation is addressed to the collectivity, the collectivity cognizant of the iconography and meaning of religious images and conversant in the language of religious narratives. Accordingly, worship comprises a joint endeavor of members of a religious collectivity, sharing a set of beliefs tied

---

5   See Fackenheim, *The Religious Dimension in Hegel's Thought*, pp. 120–22.

to shared religious narratives and shared forms of observance expressive of the piety co-religionists hold in common. In this way, religion entails religious cults, distinguished by communal practices. Here religious feeling emerges from the subjective inwardness of sentiment to obtain a worldly intersubjective reality, which involves more than just external observances by being a cult animated by the religious sentiment shared by its members. Because of this unity of inward sentiment and outward communal practice, the reality of religion cannot be produced wholly by external fiat. Religious practice must touch inner feeling and belief as well as outer communal expression, and this can be truly achieved only through the inward commitment of individuals.[6]

All the above general features of religion may seem benign as far as modernity is concerned. Yet if one considers the bases of religious diversity that lie within the common scaffold of faith, incipient conflicts appear all too possible.

The primary source for the differentiation of particular forms of religion lies in the various ways in which divinity may be represented. The absolute character and essential significance for humanity of the divine may be endemic to religion, but how these features are concretized presents options whose real embodiments distinguish the plurality of actual religions and whose succession builds the past and any future of the history of religions.

The varying representations of divinity are crucial to the relation of religion to modernity This is because how the divine is construed entails differing prescriptions of what is of fundamental value for humanity, involving differing prescriptions on how individuals should act towards divinity and one another to achieve the truth invested in the divine. To accord with modernity, religion must represent the divine in such a way that individuals' true relation to divinity entails recognition of the exclusive normativity of freedom. If the divine is instead represented in ways that challenge the supreme value of rational autonomy, religious practice will impede the realization of right that modernity brings to consummation. Insofar as the depiction of the divine represents what is

---

6 Hegel develops all these points in his account of "The Notion of Religion" in the first part of his *Lectures on the Philosophy of Religion: One Volume Edition: The Lectures of 1827*, ed. Peter Hodgson (Berkeley: University of California Press, 1988), pp. 138–97. For a concise presentation of the argument, as it bears upon the religious cult, see Fackenheim, *The Religious Dimension in Hegel's Thought*, pp. 123–5.

of absolute significance, the more divinity diverges from rational agency, the more humanity's alignment with the divine will involve a renunciation of both the institutions of freedom and the privatization of faith that secular emancipation and religious freedom involve. Although it may be historically contingent what forms of religion have arisen and continue to be practiced, the possible ways of construing the divine allow for varieties of religious faith that present very unequal challenges to modernity.

Rational Agency and the Fundamental Ways of Construing Divinity

Religion's construal of the divine always involves a conceptual underpinning and an imagined configuration that together represent what a community of believers takes the absolute to be to which they must relate to achieve right and truth.

The general problem facing particular religions is to come up with an adequate configuration for what is both transcendently absolute and absolutely important to human life. Different contents can be ascribed these dual features of divinity and the possible options might seem endless. Certainly the imagined shapes that enter religious representation have a contingent variety that cannot be determined apart from actual observation of the images and narratives that get employed in envisioning the divine. The conceptual characterization of the divine, however, is susceptible of a reasoned taxonomy that the philosophy of religion can address. So long as one attends to this conceptual element in religious representation, one can group according to type the contents that can characterize the divine, bringing some order into the possible variegation of religions.

To differentiate conceptually the possible construals of the divine, it makes sense to take rational agency as a point of reference. This is not just because modernity accords supreme value to rational autonomy in thought and action, but also because religion is always concerned with portraying an absolute that defines what rational agents should find supremely valuable. Faith can represent the divine in a spectrum from what is most independent and alien to what is closest to rational agency. The domain other to rational autonomy comprises Nature, understood as what is given on its own apart from rational agency and convention. The realization of rational autonomy can, by contrast, be understood broadly as Spirit. On these terms, the construal of the divine can be differentiated by the extent to which it involves determinations of nature as opposed to determinations of spirit.

Religion, to begin with, can simply identify the divine with nature, locating what is absolute in the realm of what is given independently of rational agency. The resulting sacralization of nature is not just a maneuver to explain the mysteries of the natural world. It comprises more deeply recognition that what is artificial and conventional is relative to human artifice and thereby an unlikely candidate for divinity.

The identification of the divine with nature has several fundamental possibilities. Divinity can be invested in particular natural objects, making them the focal point of worship and the orientation of human life. Although any specific thing, whether inorganic or organic, can be made sacred, that investiture of divine significance cannot leave the privileged objects simply as they are found. To serve the purpose of being both absolute and supremely important, such objects must be accorded features that transcend their given natural character, which is all too prosaically limited to manifest anything divine. Hence, these natural things must be regarded as somehow supernatural, for only then can individuals feel inspired to worship them and to subordinate themselves to their power. Some transfiguration is required, for the nature-worshiper does not venerate mere nature, but the divine construed as natural.[7]

Sacralized natural objects can be appropriated for magic, enlisting their supernatural powers to fulfill prosaic aims. That usage is pseudo-religious, for instead of worshiping infinitude in nature, magic subordinates what is allegedly absolute to the finite ends of individuals. Instead of magically subjecting the supernatural to human control, genuine religious worship must regard what it venerates as higher than the human and indeed, as transcending all limited concerns.[8]

Even if the temptations of magic are avoided, however, the sacred enchantment of particular natural objects poses problems for faith. Since the supernatural endowments of natural things transcend the finitude of their particular being, the rationale for privileging certain objects over any other is readily suspect. More generally, religious representation faces the dilemma of how to retain the identification of divinity and nature, without having the limitations of natural things undermine the infinity of the absolute. Religious representation is thus impelled to leave behind the immediate existence of finite natural objects and find some other natural avenues for the divine. Two options are available: divinity can be located

---

7   Fackenheim points this out in *The Religious Dimension in Hegel's Thought*, p. 186.

8   See Fackenheim, *The Religious Dimension in Hegel's Thought*, p. 120.

in general natural forces or in imagined shapes that fantastically expand upon natural entities, exaggerating their configurations, magnitude, and powers beyond all naturally given limits. Although both options provide natural forms that overcome the specific bounds of given natural objects, there still remains a discrepancy between these forms and the absolute character they are to convey. Natural powers (for example fire, thunder, rain, light, vegetative growth, and so on) may transcend any individual thing that is subject to them, but they still have a definite character that distinguishes them from both other powers and the objects that are under their sway. Because they operate in relation to what is other to them, these powers are expressly finite, defined by boundaries they can never eliminate. The same is true of any imaginatively enhanced natural things, for no matter how fantastic they be, they remain situated within a world, bounded by its general parameters and by every other object they confront.

Since no particular natural thing, nor any natural powers, nor any imaginatively magnified natural being can escape the defining limitations that leave them with a finitude at odds with any divine vocation, religious representation has one last gambit available to it if the divine is to reside in nature. Instead of privileging any particular natural factor, faith can regard the divine as being at one with nature, yet devoid of any particular limitation. The divine will overcome finitude by having no determinate character at all. It will be what is fundamental in nature, the one absolute, true reality that is afflicted by no otherness, no boundaries, no conditions. The divine is then the indeterminate nothingness, comprising the true being of nature, whose manifold finite variegation is just a phenomenal world of illusion, from which individuals must withdraw to commune with what is fundamental.[9] This option enjoins individuals to recognize the illusory character of everything set and determinate in human life. Ultimately, we are to achieve our true essence by becoming indifferent to everything individual and bounded, to every attachment of our phenomenal selves, securing unity with the absolute by somehow yielding to the same indeterminacy in which infinity is represented to reside.

Yet this nirvana still leaves unaccounted for the very phenomenality it renounces. An infinite that escapes limitation by being indeterminate

---

9   These construals are basic to the Hindu understanding of the divine as *nirguna* (devoid of quality), of the phenomenal world being *maya*, and of unity with the divine being achieved through the self-effacement of *nirvana*, notions that equally play a crucial role in the development of Buddhism and Taoism.

casts all determinacy, all finite existence into a beyond from which it has withdrawn. Not only can the indeterminate provide no principle for generating the plenitude of phenomena, but it stands limited by what it cannot contain. An indeterminate divine that excludes all finitude is bounded by a beyond of the finite which casts in jeopardy its own infinitude.

In face of these looming difficulties, it is understandable how religious representation is led to pursue a fundamentally different path, abandoning the identification of nature and the divine and instead construing the divine as spirit. This construal can take two extremes, one utilizing the natural existence of spirit and the other extricating the divine spirit from nature in its entirety.

The first option represents the divine as spirit by appropriating the natural form in which spirit exists. From our vantage point on earth, where the only naturally given intelligent agents so far encountered are human, this involves ascribing an anthropomorphic shape to the divine. Any natural configuration, human or not, however, is of one type distinguished from other types of natural things, as well as a particular example of whatever kind it is. Anthropomorphizing the divine thus renders it a particular deity among other possible anthropomorphic deities, all of whom stand conditioned by one another, as well as by whatever other natural things reside within the encompassing cosmos. Consequently, the naturally spiritualized divinities find themselves limited by their peers in a way wholly analogous to how finite rational agents stand at risk to one another. Moreover, insofar as these deities are prey to externalities, both spiritual and purely natural, beyond their control, they are subject to a fate that holds them all under its sway. The resulting polytheism taints divine spirit with a finitude, rendering it more demi-god than bearer of transcendent authority. This readily leads to a religious attitude that sees fit to use the contending deities for prosaic purposes, as ancient Roman faith did when it appropriated the ancient Greek pantheon. Such mercenary piety, however, becomes as self-defeating as the magical use of nature divinities. Gods whose spirit can be subordinated to human interests can hardly retain any supra-human power and glory.

All these difficulties might seem surmounted by the opposing option, which represents the divine as a spirit completely extricated from nature. To overcome the limits of natural existence, such divinity must be a supreme rational agency devoid of any physical presence of its own and devoid of any entanglement with any preexisting cosmos or any other disembodied deities. Relations to other purely spiritual divinities are precluded, since escaping the finitude of any natural embodiment equally deprives the divine of any means for individuating it from any other deity. Hence, the absolute cannot help but be the one and only divinity, a divinity of infinite thought and will. Yet to be a supreme will, the divine must be able to go beyond thinking about itself and realize its thought in something other. If there already existed a cosmos that stood on its own apart from the divine, there would be something beyond the divine undermining its own freedom from external limitation. Any otherness must instead be generated by a completely free resolve of the divine. Only then can the divine be more than self-thinking thought and be a supreme will. On this basis, nature emerges as a creation of the divine, who comprises its supreme lord. Such a nature will not have the structure of an artifact, composed of preexisting universal essences that inform a preexisting matter. Since neither eternal universal essences nor an eternal matter are compatible with a divine spirit that is free of any external encumbrances, nature as creation will be suitable for investigation by an empirical science that abandons the task of conceiving eternal natures of things and instead relies upon observation to apprehend the cosmos as it is contingently given.[10]

Not surprisingly, a divine that is an absolute will with no natural character will have its only image in natural rational agents, who alone among worldly things can exhibit what most approximates divinity—autonomous reason and free will. Moreover, if such a god is what humanity must relate to in order to achieve what is of supreme value, the human essence will be intimately tied to the freedom of will that the Lord supremely represents. As such, the human essence will not be defined by natural differences that set individuals in a natural inequality with respect to the divine. Instead, individuals will be equal before the divine to the degree that they all possess the same freedom of will by which they are directed to the divine. Consequently, the Lord will preeminently command individuals by law, which applies equally to all subjects, rather than by decree, whose singular command addresses particular individuals to the exclusion of others. Given divine omnipotence, the supreme Lord can, of course, subject one or just some peoples to its will, as revealed in the divine law. Since, however, those who are to submit to the divine find therein their truth and thereby share in the freedom that defines infinite spirit,

---

10 Michael B. Foster has explored this connection between the doctrine of creation and modern science in his seminal essay, "The Christian Doctrine of Creation and the Rise of Modern Natural Science" (*Mind*, vol. XLIII, 1934).

their submission should take the form of a chosen commitment, whose collective discipline replaces any natural order with one determined by will.[11] Hence, religious representation can suitably portray the adherence to divine command as a covenant with the divine to which members of a particular religious community agree to submit. Alternately, covenants with one or several peoples can be supplanted by a universal mandate to humanity at large, where the revealed command of the divine comprises a divine law that all should obey. In either case, the supreme spirit cannot be just an equal to humanity, entering into covenants whose parties are on a par. Instead of being a contractual agreement with fully mutual obligations, any covenants between God and humanity represent a divine promise to provide salvation so long as individuals choose to be faithful and obedient.[12] Only because God has freely bound himself through covenant can humanity trust in a divinity otherwise unlimited and unpredictable.[13] So long, however, as the divine will still dictates what humanity should follow, individuals are subject to a law they can never create for themselves. The law in question must be revealed, since if it were simply a product of reason, the law would not be divine in origin, but merely a dictate of the autonomous thought of any rational agent. Confronting divine revelation, individuals can at most exercise some independent prerogative in interpreting what the divine law means and how it should be implemented in particular given circumstances. Yet these initiatives do not alter the fact that the faithfuls' unification with the divine consists in essentially external observances of externally given commands, where individuals submit to edicts of the supreme Lord instead of engaging in any self-legislating autonomy.

---

11 In this respect, believers become, as Michael Walzer puts it, "bondsmen" rather than children of God. See Michael Walzer, *The Revolution of the Saints: A Study in the Origins of Radical Politics* (Cambridge, MA: Harvard University Press, 1982), p. 168.

12 As Walzer points out, insofar as human consent cannot limit the all mighty divine, covenant serves to activate those who covenant with God rather than to control God. See Walzer, *The Revolution of the Saints*, p. 167.

13 Strauss makes this point, indicating how the uncontrollable character of divine will makes intelligible how the law of one particular tribe could be *the* divine law, superior to the idolatrous conventions of other communities. See Leo Strauss, *Jewish Philosophy and the Crisis of Modernity: Essays and Lectures in Modern Jewish Thought*, ed. Kenneth Hart Green (Albany, NY: State University of New York Press, 1997), pp. 114–15.

This divide between the absolute will of the divine and the submission of humanity presents a difficulty. If the divine spirit is to represent the true essence of humanity and the divine is an absolute rational agency, can humanity attain its truth by merely obeying external commands of divine law, even when that obedience rests on covenant? The gap between infinite and finite agency seems insurmountable so long as the divine is completely extricated from nature and reigns over creation as a supreme Lord. For how can those who are subjects of a divine master be in the image of the divine who is supremely free?

An analogous problem appears to afflict human reason in its relation to the divine, seemingly setting philosophy in intractable conflict with revealed religion. If humanity is created in subservience to the external commands of the Lord, then we seem to have been given reason by God to comprehend those commands in free obedience. Yet the very autonomy of reason liberates it from any subservience to revelation, which philosophy can always call into question.[14] Admittedly, this leaves open the possibility that philosophy might autonomously confirm the truth of revelation. Revelation, however, involves contingent, historical happenings, predicated upon acts of divine will that seem fundamentally incongruent with the universal necessary truths that philosophical reason addresses. The philosopher might be tempted to suspend judgment about sacred matters that lie beyond speculative thought, but revelation concerns what supposedly is most important for human life and least amenable to suspended indifference. Yet how can the fundamental significance of revelation by certified if revelation involves an ineluctable positive element, which, if not contradicting reason at least transcends it, rendering revelation suprarational and not just derivable from reason? Unless appeal is made to reason, how can the content of alleged revelation

---

14 Strauss points to this conflict as both unresolvable and essential to the vitality of Western civilization, whose driving inner tension allegedly resides in an irremediable opposition between Jerusalem and Athens, between revealed religion and philosophy. See Strauss, *Jewish Philosophy and the Crisis of Modernity*, pp. 116–23. Ancient Greek philosophy may well be metaphysically irreconcilable with a spiritualized divine who is creator of humanity and nature, as Algazali and, more recently, Michael B. Foster have argued. Yet whether *all* philosophy is conceptually incongruent with the truths religiously represented by revealed religion is another matter. Strauss identifies philosophy with the ancient Greek search for first principles, failing to recognize that philosophy can and should emancipate itself from the foundationalism in which ancient philosophy remains trapped.

be distinguished from artifacts of human irrationality? Yet by demanding that revelation prove itself before the tribunal of reason, does philosophy not take for granted what revelation denies, that the truth of revelation depends on human reason rather than God's will?[15]

These parallel difficulties elicit a religious remedy, where faith represents a bridging of the divide between the divine spirit and finite agency. This bridging cannot just consist in immediately identifying the divine with either one or all finite rational agents. If one actual person is revered as God, the results are as ludicrous as Roman emperor worship, where an all too finite personality is slavishly treated as an absolute tyrant. On the other hand, if some or all persons are regarded as divine, the limits of polytheism enter with a vengeance, for now the pantheon of deities has been brought down to earth, erasing any godly transcendence.

The problem at hand has a logical core that haunts all attempts at religious representation: the infinite cannot sustain its overcoming of finitude if it remains opposed to the finite as something irretrievably beyond. To avoid reverting to finitude, the infinite must not relate to the finite as something lying outside it. Instead, the infinite must contain the finite, but in such a way as not to be reducible to it. The infinite must relate to itself in relating to the finite, while the finite must equally relinquish its opposition to the infinite. In religious terms this signifies that the divine must relate to finite human agency as a form of itself, just as that finite human agency must cancel its separation from the divine, transcending the limits of mortality. Religious representation is not restricted to any one narrative or set of images to construe the divine that becomes human and the human that transcends its own finitude in uniting with divinity. Nevertheless, Christianity, with its doctrine of the Trinity and the passion of Christ, presents one possible embodiment of this construal. The distinguishing dogma is that the divine becomes an actual finite individual, who must die and be resurrected to transcend mortality and reunite with divinity. The resurrection need not be understood as a tangible occurrence susceptible of historical verification, raising all the paradoxes that Kierkegaard dissects in his *Concluding Unscientific Postscript*.[16] Rather the reuniting of man and god can be a resurrection for faith dwelling in the spirit of the religious community that honors the infinity

---

15 Strauss lays out these difficulties in *Jewish Philosophy and the Crisis of Modernity*, pp. 121–2, 127–8.

16 Søren Kierkegaard, *Concluding Unscientific Postscript*, trans. David F. Swenson and Walter Lowrie (Princeton, NJ: Princeton University Press, 1968).

of human freedom.[17] Yet, insofar as the form of representation remains an essential feature of religion, the combination of inward accessibility and transcendence persists, leaving believers wavering between devotional unity with the "indwelling Christ" and the historical representation "which sends him back two thousand years into Palestine."[18] In any event, insofar as the divine gets here represented as overcoming the divide of infinite and finite, personal initiative can be empowered to play a central role in doctrinal interpretation and in setting the paths that worship and religious fellowship should take. Medieval Catholicism may put off the reconciliation of infinite and finite to an otherworldly beyond, leaving human dignity unrecognized in the prosaic present of feudal bondage. Yet, when the reconciliation is acknowledged in the here and now, as heralded in the Protestant Reformation, the implications for worldly freedom become more consistently manifest, both in the supplanting of ecclesiastical hierarchy by personal conscience and in the embrace of civil society and self-government.

If this reconciles human and divine will, it also allows reason to make peace with revelation. Once the normativity of theory is recognized to reside in the fully self-responsible autonomy of reason, the free will can be known to be the rational will, and reason need no longer oppose the positivity of freedom, be it divine or human. Revelation may retain aspects irreducible to reason, given the essential requirement that religious representation be imagined and not just thought. Still, at its core, revealed religion will now have made manifest the same truth of humanity that philosophy conceives.

Whether the accomplished reconciliation of the divine and the human requires any further relation *to* the divine is a question that individuals are left to consider as they enjoy autonomy sanctioned by a faith that removes the last barrier separating the finite from the infinite.

The preceding sketch of how religions can construe the divine[19] may already suggest a diversity in compatibility with modernity's embrace of

---

17 As Stephen Houlgate observes, discussing Hegel's analysis of Christian dogma, Christ is resurrected not just for faith, but *as* faith, as the spirit of love guiding the religious community. See Houlgate, *An Introduction to Hegel: Freedom, Truth and History* (Oxford: Blackwell Publishing, 2005), p. 267.

18 See Fackenheim, *The Religious Dimension in Hegel's Philosophy*, p. 186, who here quotes Hegel.

19 With one addition, this sketch of the differentiation of religious construals of the divine largely fits Western philosophy's most ambitious and systematic attempt to conceive the particular forms of religion—Hegel's *Lectures on*

self-determination. To substantiate that diversity, however, it is necessary to consider the specific requirements of the different spheres of freedom and how these may collide with religious practice. Accordingly, we must proceed to investigate how religion relates to property rights, morality, household autonomy, civil society, and self-government.

Religion and Property Rights

Property rights comprise the most basic arena of self-determination since unless individuals respect one another's ownership of their own bodies, persons are subject to enslavement precluding their exercise of any other rights. In order for individuals to determine themselves as owners, an external domain must be present that does not comprise the reality of some other agency. Only then can individuals give their will an external reality that accords with, rather than violates, others' self-determination as owners. Nature must therefore be disenchanted if individuals are to be able to embody their wills in some external factor that can be recognized by others as the receptacle of their entitled self-determination as owner. If instead, nature is regarded as invested with spirit or spirits, individuals have no external reality divested of will in which they can rightfully objectify their own volition and achieve the recognition as owner without which no other exercise of freedom is possible. Accordingly, any religion that construes the divine as nature, worshiping natural powers and treating the natural environment as sacred and invested with spirit, deprives humanity of any room for self-determination. Under the thrall of this most abject form of religion, individuals subordinate themselves to a divine with which they can unite only by forsaking every iota of entitled independence and bowing down to powers of nature completely alien to rational agency. Faith here takes a form verging on superstition, allowing magical forces to rule every aspect of human destiny. Such religion has its counterpart in a community organized wholly in terms of kinship and other naturally conditioned factors. This precludes the universal ties of right from having any entry, for rights involve entitlements that all rational

---

the Philosophy of Religion. That addition consists in the form of religion that represents the divine as an absolute will whose commands are directed not at one chosen people, but at all humanity. This form, which we shall see is exemplified by Islam, is ignored by Hegel, although in his *Lectures on the Philosophy of History*, he provides a brief but telling account of the Islamic civilization that elaborates on this form.

agents have, no matter what else distinguishes them by birth. These "primitive" communities may provide anthropology with its privileged subject matter for investigating human nature, but that is only because communities organized around nature worship and kinship bonds order themselves in function of natural features, where differences one is born with decisively dictate how one should live. Anthropologists have shown comparatively little interest in communities governed by relations of right, since there members give themselves a self-determined character, preempting the givens of human nature from ordering their conduct.

Property rights first become coherently possible for religious individuals once the divine they worship distinguishes itself from given nature. Only then is a disenchanted external domain available for giving the free will a recognized embodiment that does not infringe upon the property of another. If, however, property rights are to extend to all competent agents, in conformity with the *right*, rather than *privilege* of ownership, the divine must further be freed of any natural distinctions that would enable birthright to determine an individual's proximity to what is of absolute value. So long as hereditary ranks prescribe what opportunities individuals may have, they cannot equally enjoy the basic freedom to take ownership and freely dispose of their property. To preclude natural differences from curtailing the freedom from enslavement, the divine must be construed as spirit, liberated from nature. Otherwise, humanity locates its true essence in a divine still defined by nature, leaving human existence ruled by factors given independently of rational autonomy, obstructing the universal right to determine oneself as an owner of property, the right on which all others depend.

Religion and Morality

The entitlements of moral accountability impose yet greater demands upon religion. The freedom of morality requires that subjects be held responsible only for what they do on purpose and only for those consequences of their purposive actions that they intend. If instead individuals are blamed for what is inadvertently caused by them or their property, they may retain recognition as owners, but not as morally responsible subjects. They may be held liable for their torts, that is, for damages they unknowingly or accidentally commit, including damages caused by what is theirs and for whose effects they can be held accountable. Nonetheless, unless their purpose and intention are recognized to circumscribe their responsibility, their moral rights go unrecognized. This sets the stage for condemning individuals without consideration of their purposes and intentions, allowing morally innocent individuals to be killed as victims of terrorism or to be exterminated en masse for being born into the wrong race or social group.

Moral autonomy, however, does not just involve rights of purpose and intention. It further extends a right of conscience to individuals, entitling and obliging them to determine the content of the moral good for whose realization they hold themselves accountable. Morality may not be the last word on freedom, given how conscience must always struggle to determine an objectively valid good with subjective resources. On occasion, individuals may find that what their conscience determines to be right coincides with what others conscientiously decide should be done. Because each conscience must decide on its own what is the good, any such coincidence is but an accident. When no such luck is to be found, moral agents fall into a quandary. Either they sanction the conscience of others while relinquishing the authority of their own conflicting conscience, or they stay true to what they determine to be right and ignore the equal claims of other conscientious agents. This quandary can only be resolved in ethical institutions of freedom, where individuals exercise roles where how they determine themselves automatically involves a harmony of end reproducing the same association to which they all belong. This is exemplified most grandly in self-government, where free citizens determine themselves in such a manner that exercising their constitutional rights insures that they do not violate the constitutional political activity of others, but rather contribute to upholding the regime of political self-determination in which they participate. Although morality lacks this guaranteed harmony of ends, it provides the only valid avenue for self-determined conduct in the interstices untouched by the ethical obligations of family, civil, and political association. There, where no guidance is offered by standing laws or existing associations of freedom, individuals have only their own conscience to fall back upon if they are not to subject themselves to external powers.

Religion can respect moral autonomy only by according individuals two coordinate religious freedoms - the freedom to choose one's own faith and the freedom to interpret one's creed without subjection to clerical authority. Under these allowances, individuals can subscribe to their faith in complete conformity with their freedom of conscience. What they believe in will then be a good whose content they have freely ascertained and which they freely embrace. If a religion instead compels adherence to a doctrine of the good whose interpretation is imposed upon its followers by a clerical hierarchy, moral autonomy is doubly violated. To accord with moral autonomy, the divine cannot be a tyrant, to whom selfless servitude is required, either directly or through submission to religious officials. The divine must be such as to be encountered only through a voluntary subscription to faith, empowering individuals to interpret personally the religion to which they adhere. Otherwise faith will violate moral right, no matter what it may prescribe.

Religion and Household Rights

Household emancipation, for its part, requires that individuals be free to marry without restriction to religious affiliation, race, sexual orientation, or any other factor irrelevant to the ability to observe the rights and duties of conjugal relations. If instead a religion refuses to sanctify interfaith marriage or demands conversion of an infidel spouse, or otherwise imposes restrictions upon marital freedom and the equality of spouses, it will obstruct household self-determination, which is itself a precondition of social and political emancipation.[20] Unless spouses are accorded equal rights to codetermine their life together, in respect of their status as persons and moral subjects, and in respect of the corollary rights of others, marriage will hinder equal participation in social and political life. So long as a religion sanctions the domination of one spouse by another, that domination will transfer itself into society and state and ensure that the subordinate spouse will be underprivileged in those spheres as well. The same considerations apply to parental rights and duties to bring up children to autonomy. These entitlements and obligations will be violated if a religion in any way mandates care and education of children that deprives them of what they need to function as autonomous persons, moral agents, spouses and parents, members of civil society, and citizens. In this regard, religion must not stand in the way of parents providing their children a proper secular education, including exposure to other faiths. If instead a religion requires subjecting children exclusively to religious instruction, where rote repetition of sacred texts comes at the expense of other learning, faith will violate the basic parental obligation to provide children with the knowledge and skills they need to exercise their rights.

---

20 A case in point of how religious sanctification of marriage can compromise marital duty is provided by the Koran (2:220), which privileges a sexual affair with a slave who believes in Islam over marriage with an idol worshiper. See George Anastaplo, *But Not Philosophy* (Lanham, MD: Lexington Books, 2002), p. 188.

Given how family relations generally impinge upon the transmission of wealth, culture, opportunity, and the very reproduction of the populace, the consequences are far reaching whenever a religion takes control over determining who can marry according to whether the parties accede to a certain religious dogma. As Rousseau observes, the religious order then ultimately decides upon the disposal of household inheritance as well as the very population on which rest society and the state.[21] An extreme example is provided by strains of traditional Islamic law, under whose reign a born Muslim who converts to another religion will have his marriage voided, his children taken away to be raised by Muslims, his rights of inheritance forfeited, and his very life surrendered for apostasy.[22]

Generally, the more a religion construes the divine as incongruent with rational agency, the more likely it will prescribe family relations diverging from household autonomy. When, for example, nature is sacrelized, individuals will more likely find their marital and parental options defined by kinship relations, gender differences, and other factors given by birth rather than mutual choice.

Religion and Civil Society

The economic, legal, and cultural rights of civil society pose yet further challenges to religious belief and practice. To be compatible with equal economic opportunity, the related freedoms of occupation and consumption, and the due process of equal legal standing, religion must free its creed of all sanction of social hierarchies defined by birth and natural differences. The equal opportunity of civil freedom becomes incongruent with salvation when, for example, a religion construes unification with the divine as an overcoming of individual subjectivity, proceeding through reincarnations where previous lives have their value registered in differently ranked stations of rebirth.

Decisive for congruence with civil freedom is the degree to which a religion can recognize the authority of civil law, which mandates the legal enforcement of the property, household, and social rights of individuals, including their rights to due process in civil courts. Respecting civil law requires religions to relinquish any hegemonic claims for sacred law.

---

21 J.-J. Rousseau, *The Social Contract and other later political writings*, ed. Victor Gourevitch (Cambridge, UK: Cambridge University Press, 1997), p. 151.

22 Ibn Warraq, *Why I Am Not A Muslim* (Amherst, NY: Prometheus Books, 1995), p. 174.

Instead, religions must accept that submission to sacred edict be voluntary, applying only to whoever chooses to follow the creed. Making religious law a private matter, however, is only part of the reformation mandated by civil society. To be fully congruent with civil law, the voluntarily accepted sacred law must also shape its edicts so as not to violate the rights legalized in a proper civil code. Only then can a religion fit within the association of civil freedom, wherein it can coexist with other religions provided they have reformed themselves in the same manner.

Religion and Self-Government

The reformation of religion securing conformity with civil society has direct political ramifications. Insofar as religious law must be privatized to uphold household and social freedom, religion must be strictly separated from state power.

This separation is mandated not just because religious rule subverts household and civil autonomy, which are themselves bulwarks of equal political opportunity. The separation is required by the very functioning of self-government.

Self-government has four cardinal features, which imply one another: the identity of ruler and ruled, the reflexivity of governing, the universality of the form and content of political activity, and the supremacy of politics over all other spheres of practice.[23]

Unless ruler and ruled are the same, self-government will give way to domination by a political elite of a subject class, captive to an order that it does not impose upon itself. The identity of ruler and ruled cannot, however, be immediate, as advocates of direct democracy, binding mandates, and government by referenda and plebiscite mistakenly believe. Under all such schemes that attempt to make the general will of the state directly identical with the will of each citizen, political diversity gets annulled, legislative debate becomes a meaningless exercise, and political participation becomes monopolized by a class of political clones freed from all other non-political responsibilities. If any political dissension exists, no state action can be in direct unity with the will of all citizens, since the choice of some will conflict with whatever government does.

---

23 See Richard Dien Winfield, *The Just State: Rethinking Self-Government* (Amherst, NY: Humanity Books, 2005) for a detailed investigation of these cardinal features of self-government and their implications for the structure of self-government.

Real legislative deliberation is no less precluded, for any initiative by legislators to persuade or be persuaded, reach legislative compromises, or formulate laws not already fully specified in prior electoral campaigns will diverge from the will of the electorate, as expressed in the preceding election of representatives. Similarly, direct democracy will depend upon participants' full engagement in governance, which will only achieve immediate identity of ruler and ruled if all participating citizens act with unanimity and no other functions of life need be taken care of by non-participating drones. Representative democracy escapes these dilemmas by enabling the identity of ruler and ruled to be mediated by elected lawmakers, who allow all citizens to share indirectly in self-rule. Representatives achieve this so long as they exercise an autonomy to deliberate and legislate in behalf of the entire citizenry rather than for the sake of the exclusive interests of particular classes, regions, ethnic groups, or any other sectarian grouping. Then, whatever gets constitutionally legislated will be for the political good of all and mediated by the will of the entire citizenry.

So long as representative democracy secures the mediated identity of ruler and ruled, governing exhibits reflexivity, where a constitutionally organized citizenry acts upon itself. That self-activity of democratic politics is necessarily universal in respect to both content and form, for self-government is rule by the entire citizenry upon the whole, imposing an order that extends across the body politic without limitation to any particular sphere. Since this order comprises the continual sustaining of the exercise of political freedom in face of changing circumstances, the end of self-government is perennially a universal aim, none other than the realization of the political autonomy of all citizens, whose achievement consists in the universal engagement in self-governing of the entire citizenry. If instead, the end of governing is some special interest, citizens are subjected to a particular aim emanating from a particular interested party, subverting the identity of ruler and ruled and the reflexivity of governance.

For this very reason, the activity of self-government must reign supreme over all other affairs. The moment politics gets subordinated to the realization of some other end, the citizenry forfeits its autonomy as a self-governing community, becoming bound to a purpose issuing from some other agency that now imposes its particular end upon the body politic. At one blow, the identity of ruler and ruled, the reflexivity of governance, and the universality of the form and content of political action are subverted.

Preventing this outcome by retaining the supremacy of politics does not, however, leave self-government indifferent to upholding the non-political rights of property, morality, household membership, and civil society. If these had to be secured as an *external* restraint upon self-government, the rights of these pre-political practices would conflict with the supremacy of self-rule. Because, however, the identity of ruler and ruled requires equal political opportunity, securing the property, moral, family, and social rights of individuals is a precondition of the reflexivity of self-government. Any deficit in the property rights, moral recognition, family entitlements, and civil rights of citizens will impose obstacles to their equal access to political participation. Accordingly, guaranteeing the equal opportunities of citizens as owners, moral subjects, family members, and economic and legal agents is not a restriction upon self-government, but a constitutive task that a free citizenry must continually fulfill in order to enjoy the equal political opportunity necessary for self-government.

These fundamental features of political freedom might seem to leave religion unperturbed. After all, self-government cannot be consistently upheld if religious affiliation in any way conditions political participation or enjoyment of the pre-political freedoms that make equal political opportunity possible. Any privileging or underprivileging of individuals on the basis of their religion undermines the equal opportunity basic to every right, imposing religiously prejudiced hierarchies that subvert the identity of ruler and ruled, the reflexivity of governing, the universality of political ends, and the supremacy of politics. Just as official recognition of any particular faith subordinates politics to a religious dogma, whose particular group aims then reign supreme at the expense of self-rule, so complete toleration of religion would seem to be required for sustaining the unimpeded exercise of political just as much as property, moral, household, and social rights.

Yet emancipating politics and the other spheres of right from religious favoritism can only be equivalent to an unlimited political toleration of religion if religious practice is incapable of obstructing self-government and the pre-political freedoms on which it rests. Since religions vary in construing the divine and how conduct must be correspondingly molded to achieve salvation, different faiths can pose very different challenges to the flourishing of political freedom.

To be compatible with self-government as well as civil society and the non-oppressive family organization facilitating political freedom, religion must doubly restrict its own practice.

On the one hand, religion must withdraw from the political sphere, renouncing the imposition of sacred law upon the body politic, as well as society and the household, while granting its practitioners the right to interpret independently their own faith. If instead, a religion steadfastly asserts itself as a whole way of life, reigning supreme over political, social, family, and all other cultural affairs, it will obliterate the secular space enabling individuals to enjoy their autonomy as self-governing citizens, exercising the civil freedom, household liberties, and moral independence that only become possible when religion has retreated into the private arena of particular voluntary association. Even if all citizens share the same faith, subordinating the state, society, and the family to religious edict will deprive everyone of the right to govern themselves independently, together with their social rights of occupation and need and their household rights to marry whom they choose and raise children to autonomy without subjection to an unquestionable religious dogma.

On the other hand, the duly privatized religion must adopt an ecumenical toleration of other correlatively privatized religions. To do so, every religion must acknowledge the freedom of belief of all individuals, allowing them to choose their own faith (or none at all), an entitlement that requires equally granting them authority to interpret the faith of their choice as they see fit. Otherwise, two facets of freedom presupposed by self-government are precluded: moral autonomy and the religious freedom consonant with political, social, and household autonomy. If clerical authority deprives individuals of the right to interpret their creed and the ultimate ends it imposes upon humanity, they will lose the moral right to determine the good that they should bring about through their action, a right that underlies the freedom of citizens to determine what political program they should promote. Consequently, any clerical monopoly of religious interpretation is inconsistent with not only ecumenical toleration of other faiths and of their right to proselytize, but the rights of citizens to determine what good the state should strive to achieve.

Above all, what self-government cannot tolerate is the entry of religious organizations into the political sphere to seek power. The moment political parties are permitted to identify themselves in terms of any sectarian interest, be it defined by religion, region, ethnicity, race, language, class, or gender, they forfeit the universality of form and content that alone allows parties to escape the pernicious factionalism that subverts self-rule. If, for example, a religious sect is allowed to field a political party of its own and vie for political power, the reflexivity of self-government will face annulment at the hands of rule by one faith's members over everyone else. Not only will this permit government to fall into the clutches of a particular faction from which citizens at large are excluded, but it will enable religious law to be imposed over society and household, destroying the secular equal opportunities of civil society and the emancipated family on which self-government depends. Unless parties are open in principle to all citizens and distinguish themselves by properly political differences on how to promote the political, social, and household freedoms of all in face of current circumstances, government will become hijacked by particular factions, whose representation of a special interest guarantees the perversion of self-rule into the dominion of one group over a subject class including everyone else. Accordingly, self-government structurally requires the banning of all religious political parties. Political freedom also requires the exclusion from office-holding of all clerics who do not resign their religious positions, so long as retention of religious posts jeopardizes the secular independence and universality of self-government.

The Algerian and Turkish military authorities were therefore right to annul elections about to be captured by religious parties, but wrong to have allowed such parties in the first place. Blocking religious groups from gaining entry into the political sphere is as much a bulwark of civil society, household emancipation, and general cultural freedom as it is of self-government. The same is true of prohibiting fascist and Stalinist movements from contesting elections. Because one cannot have a right to conspire to destroy the institutions of freedom, democracy cannot consistently tolerate anti-democratic parties, be they religious or secular.

The only exceptions to these exclusions are transitional situations of historic compromise, where the weakness of secular parties and traditional oppressions at home and in society make it impossible to gain sufficient support for emerging institutions of freedom without yielding on the admittance of religious groups into the political arena. Such admissions, however, are permissible only insofar as they provide transitional accommodations advancing towards the full realization of self-government, which cannot be ultimately achieved without the completed privatization of religion.[24]

Even in their most unyielding form, the measures for ensuring the thoroughgoing separation of religion from politics are far from being

---

24 As we shall see, such compromises served their emancipatory purpose in Turkey under Mustafa Kemal, and may perhaps serve their purpose in the attempted democratic transformations under way in Afghanistan and Iraq.

impositions upon religion. Rather, they comprise the fundamental prerequisite for freedom of belief, a freedom enabling privatized, ecumenical faiths to flourish without religious compromise.

For this reason, the separation of religion from politics need not lead to unceasing intestine conflicts, such as Rousseau claims afflict Christendom, ever since Jesus invoked an other-worldly kingdom, divorcing the City of God from the City of Man, and introducing dual loyalties that jeopardize political unity.[25] The question of whether to obey magistrate or priest is only unresolvable when jurisdictions conflict. Certainly Christ sees an absence of collision when he enjoins us to "render unto Caesar the things which are Caesar's and unto God the things which are God's" (Matthew 22:17). The perpetual strife that Rousseau presumes only occurs if religious authority rejects, and indeed, must reject, the privatization of faith and the binding validity of civil law. Significantly, Rousseau sees Islam escaping divergent loyalties by joining religion and rule, forging under the Caliphs a government strictly united with respect to faith and political authority.[26] Political unity may be good, provided the state is such as to be worth upholding. The normatively valid political unity of self-government cannot be realized, however, when one sacred dogma directly reigns at the expense of self-legislation and religious freedom.

Admittedly, as Rousseau insists, it does matter to the state that citizens subscribe to religions that make them devoted, rather than antipathetic to their civic duties.[27] As he himself recognizes, this occurs only insofar as faith honors the freedoms that citizens are due. For this reason, the civil religion that Rousseau introduces to bind citizens together restricts its dogma to upholding morality and the duties of good citizens, providing sentiments of sociability that conform to political freedom. Any further impositions would introduce a pernicious intolerance to opposing behavior, making it impossible for citizens to live in peace with one another or with any foreigners they believe to be intolerable infidels.[28] In effect, the civil religion becomes politically redundant, reducing to a conviction to uphold right, a conviction that can be held with purely secular respect for the normativity of freedom.

---

25 See Rousseau, *The Social Contract and other later political writings*, pp. 144–5.

26 Rousseau, *The Social Contract and other later political writings*, p. 145.

27 Rousseau, *The Social Contract and other later political writings*, p. 150.

28 Rousseau, *The Social Contract and other later political writings*, p. 151.

Of course, the mere separation of religion and politics is no guarantee that government actualizes political freedom. As Arendt points out, political freedom is not just to "Render unto Caesar what is Caesar's and unto God what is God's," but to exercise the right to codetermine those affairs that once were Caesar's.[29] For this reason, the Christian demarcation of secular and sacred spheres can signify merely a freedom *from* politics, allowing Christian slaves to find salvation and Christian churches to refrain from denouncing slavery while holding all equal before God.[30] Nonetheless, if equality before God is joined to a respect for freedom and responsibility, exclusion from self-government gets hard to sustain coherently. Once all are acknowledged to be equally *free* before God, political emancipation becomes imperative.

Certainly, so long as a religion resists the doctrinal reforms that may be necessary to become compatible with moral autonomy and secular rights, it will be unable consistently to respect freedom of belief and the self-government ecumenical toleration makes possible. This does not mean that a recalcitrant religion must be proscribed by democracy. Given the possibility of reinterpreting religious texts and traditions, it is never the creed itself that warrants prohibition. Instead, what is required is only that a religion's hegemonic practices be constrained within the privatized limits of civil society, forcing its faithful to be observant of the rights of others while enjoying their own duly lawful religious freedom.

The Internal Imperative for Religious Reformation

All the above requirements that religions must satisfy to accord with the institutions of freedom might seem to be external compromises imposed by a modernity essentially alien to religious concerns. Certainly the foundation-free character of self-determination alone entails that modernity's system of right stands in need no more of a religious than of any other foundation, even if religions must be of a certain character so as not to obstruct modern freedoms.

Nonetheless, the imperative to shape religious belief and practice to accord with the exclusive normativity of self-determination is wholly immanent to religion. Instead of coming from without, the identification of freedom and value is a fundamentally religious concern because religion, to be worthy of the name, seeks in our relation to the divine what is of

---

29   Arendt, *Essays in Understanding 1930–1954*, p. 373.
30   Arendt, *Essays in Understanding 1930–1954*, p. 373.

essential importance to humanity. Any assignment of fundamental worth to a religiously sanctioned oppression falls prey to the same dilemmas of foundational justification that afflict any secular appeal to foundations. By now, the problem is all too familiar. So long as a valid life owes its character to something external, instead of to its own self-determination, what confers validity remains separate from what possesses validity. As a result, the foundation that allegedly bestows validity upon humanity cannot meet its own standard, which consists in being determined by the privileged ground it comprises. To function as the foundation of validity, this ground constitutively determines something other than itself. If the privileged foundation were to determine itself, which it must do to satisfy its own validity requirement and become self-referentially consistent, the defining difference between foundation and what is founded would collapse, leaving validity consisting in what is self-determined. Accordingly, the exclusive normativity of self-determination need not depend upon any external assumptions. Any attempt to offer an alternative automatically treats what is valid as owing its validity to something other than itself, resurrecting foundational justification, which, on its own terms, demands eliminating the distinction between foundation and validated practice, leaving self-determination as the only possible bearer of normativity.

Consequently, if religion is to be true to its own vocation and locate the truth of humanity in its relation to the divine, divinity must be so construed that humanity's relation to it entails the emancipation of humanity. To be a law expressing the divine's true prescriptions to humanity, religious law must be a law of freedom, allowing individuals to worship and belong to their religious community without impeding the exercise of their rights as owners, moral subjects, free and equal spouses and parents, members of civil society, and self-governing citizens. As we have seen, this entails granting individuals religious freedom, empowering them to decide independently what their faith will be, and obliging them to respect others' entitlement to do the same. Religion can include observances distinct from the general strictures of secular law provided that any such ritual practice not violate the rights of individuals at home, in society, or in political community.

The resulting privatization of religion and ecumenical tolerance might appear to involve a self-defeating concession to religious relativism, fatally undermining religion's own constitutive claim to locate the absolute truth of humanity in relation to the absolute. This would be true for any religion that construes the divine such that worship and religious practice imprisons humanity in a community of subservience. If, however, religion represents the divine in conformity with what is justifiably of value in human life, the acceptance of religious freedom does not devalue religious doctrine. Instead, it only confirms the exclusive validity of the religious doctrine whose divinity prescribes human emancipation. So long as a religion recognizes that faith should be freely adopted and that religious practice should not oppress its faithful, the toleration of other creeds and the acceptance of secular institutions of freedom need present no compromise of the exclusive truth of any duly reformed religion. For this reason, the modernization of religion is not a recipe for relativizing faith and undermining the appeal of religion. Modernity is fully congruent with religion so long as religion consummates itself on its own terms. What de Tocqueville observed in the juvenile United States was not the flourishing of every sort of religious practice, but a cornucopia of religions that had sufficiently modernized themselves to coexist without forsaking their own creed.

Although religions widely vary with respect to how much they must reform their dogma, observances, and hierarchy to become congruent with the civilization of freedom, all possess the capability of reinterpreting their creed to make it more compatible with modernity. Fundamentalists may wish to uphold their own authority and repress religious freedom by laying claim to an unambiguous literal reading of their holy scriptures. Nevertheless, no scripture interprets itself, even if the basis of interpretation always lies in common understandings that make communication possible. Reinterpretation of prevailing dogma must retain some recognizable connection to religious tradition in order to comprise a religious reformation, rather than a revolutionary founding of a new faith. This requirement, however, leaves religious reformers otherwise free to reshape their faith in greater conformity with the institutions of freedom. Because religion seeks in the divine what is of absolute value for humanity and absolute value can lie nowhere else but in self-determination, theologians can always make a case for embracing ecumenical privatization and secular freedom as a consummation of absolute religious truth, rather than a sacrifice of faith to relativism.

This holds true whether a religion has a revealed dogma or not. Divine revelation may claim authority simply on the basis of its absolute source, but this claim can never rule out religious reform. Whatever is alleged to be revealed, divine law can always be questioned with regard to both its authenticity and its meaning. Believers may simply hold fast to their faith that putative revelation emanates from the divine and that what it commands is self-evident. Yet so long as believers can think, they can always ask what it is that guarantees the authority of the privileged texts, especially when confronted with competing religions that lay claim to other would-be revelations and dogmas. Even if the question of authenticity is never raised, the meaning of revelation can still become a matter of debate among the faithful. On either front, the raising of questions introduces the need for justification, which raises the problem of finding authenticating foundations, a problem whose resolution leads to recognizing the normativity of self-determination. Believers in revealed religion might object that revelation must contribute something more than what reason independently establishes, since otherwise, revelation becomes superfluous, casting into doubt the need to have any relation to the divine. Yet this objection is itself an engagement in argument that, as such, must confront questions of validity. There is no closing of the door to reason to help support religious dogma and clarify what it should mean.

Indeed, the very appeal to reason can have no occasion but belief. In the *Apology*, Socrates could claim that the gods command him to engage in self-examination,[31] for the urge to philosophize can hardly have a basis in reason. Any rational ground for appealing to reason would fall prey to the vicious circularity of presupposing some of the rational wisdom that philosophy seeks to obtain. On the other hand, without the holding of beliefs, there is nothing to question and without the questioning there can be no recognition of one's ignorance, from which the quest for wisdom can genuinely begin. This does not render what and how philosophy thinks relative to a will to believe or an irrational choice to privilege reason.[32] Philosophy cannot begin from any determining ground, since any such foundation would then be taken for granted, making philosophy subservient to unjustified opinion. Instead, philosophical thought must establish its own method and subject matter in the course of its own self-examination. Belief and will may occasion the resolve to think philosophically, but neither can determine what should be thought and thereby serve as a juridical foundation of reason. Because reason must

---

31 Plato, *Apology*, 23b, in Plato, *Complete Works*, ed. John Cooper (Indianapolis: Hackett Publishing Company, 1997), p. 22.

32 Strauss, like Kierkegaard, holds that the choice of philosophy is based on an unevident premise, rendering philosophy incapable of establishing its own necessity (Strauss, *Jewish Philosophy and the Crisis of Modernity*, p. 131). This would be true only if justification must be foundational, always appealing to first principles or some other privileged given to confer validity. As we have seen, foundational justification undermines itself by its own attempt to be self-referentially consistent, leaving normativity residing in self-determination.

determine its own itinerary in order to legitimate itself, philosophy can have no foundations.

Religion and Modernization

The demands that modernity puts before every religion may always be fulfillable through religious reform, but that does not prevent different religions from being more or less of an obstacle to modernization. One of the most striking features of the war on terrorism is that the Jihad waged by Islamists roots itself in a religious tradition which, wherever it has predominated, has centered nations that have failed to modernize themselves. Whatever power and glory Muslim empires may have once enjoyed, with the advent of modernity in another cultural milieu, the Islamic world has lost its preeminence and become subject to an external modernization imposed through colonialism and imperialism. As a result, the contemporary world of Islam is mostly a post-colonial realm, mired in all the difficulties endemic to the post-colonial condition.

To comprehend this situation and its implications for the war on Islamist terrorism, one must first examine the dynamic of modernization, as both internally and externally generated. Only then will it be possible to consider what responsibility Islam may bear for the pervasive failure of predominantly Muslim nations to develop independently the institutions of modern freedom, as well as what should be done to overcome that failure.

Chapter 4

Modernity and the Post-Colonial Condition

The Problem of Post-Colonialism

Amidst the euphoria greeting the end of the Cold War, the temptation has been great to welcome a new world order heralding the global triumph of democracy and free enterprise with a human face. Following fascism's defeat a half century before, the sudden collapse of super power rivalry has relieved much of the totalitarian challenge to civil society and constitutional self-government. Yet celebrating the completed march of reason in history remains premature. While daunting problems still plague the transition from communism to capitalism as well as capitalist democracy itself, another unresolved opposition looms ever larger, an opposition fatefully underlying, if not identical with that of the war on terrorism. While the world stage has been commandeered by a past century of inter-imperialist, fascist/anti-fascist, and communist/capitalist slaughter, the great majority of humanity has undergone a different ordeal. Traced by overlapping rubrics of colonialism, Westernization, modernization, and development, and culminating in the political liberations creating the post-colonial condition, this parallel history can no longer lie outside the limelight.

Both as an external opposition between North and South, the developed and the underdeveloped, or the West and its other, and as an internal opposition within post-colonial society, a chapter of history is unfolding, distinctly different from the birth of the modern that left and right Hegelians once viewed as the final combat. How is this development to be understood? Can the categories with which the master thinkers of modernity comprehended our age grasp the post-colonial predicament and shed light on the war on Islamist terrorism?

The problem at issue has key descriptive elements, most important of which concerns the contingent or non-contingent character of how Western nations modernized themselves while non-Western nations were generally subjected to a "Westernization" imposed through the yoke of colonial and imperial domination. Above all, however, what lies at stake is prescriptive inquiry. To guide our conduct in face of the most pressing practical issues of today, we must first examine the normativity of modernity and of the Western developments initially giving rise to modern institutions. Then, we must extend our investigation to probe the separability of modernization and Westernization, the legitimacy of imposing modern institutions from without, and finally the normative tensions within post-colonial societies and between developed and underdeveloped nations.

All of these normative questions are decided as much by how modernity is understood, as by how normativity is itself conceived. To set the stage, key arguments presented earlier must be rehearsed. Defenders and detractors alike generally agree that modernity distinguishes itself from prior forms of civilization by calling into question given tradition and demanding that practices and institutions command legitimacy only to the degree that they are justified by reason. Hence, the institutions that modernity erects putatively in accord with reason lay claim to a universality reflecting their independence of the contingent particulars of given authority. Not surprisingly, the distinctively modern institutions that are understood to be universally valid are institutions of freedom, determined not by their conformity to particular ancestral tradition, but by their realization of self-determination. The institutions giving reality to self-determination can qualify as the real that is rational precisely because freedom exhibits the independence from foundations that reason must exhibit if it is to provide any justification that does not rely upon dogmatically accepted criteria, rules, procedures of construction, or any other privileged vocabularies. Precisely because free institutions do not draw their legitimacy from any conformity to given tradition, they can only be justified by a reasoning that rejects the traditional view that justification amounts to derivation from some foundation. Thus, to decry the failure of the Enlightenment to establish foundations for modern autonomy[1] is not to expose any crack in the facade of modernity, nor to unmask limits in reason. Rather, the very failure to locate foundations for modernity is indicative of how the universality of modernity's institutions of freedom involves their independence from all prior grounds.[2]

---

1   For an example of this misguided critique of the Enlightenment, see Alasdair MacIntyre, *After Virtue* (Notre Dame, IN: University of Notre Dame Press, 1981), p. 49 ff.

2   For a powerful development of this point, see William Maker, *Philosophy Without Foundations: Rethinking Hegel* (Albany, NY: State University of New York Press, 1994), pp. 21–45.

It is the universality of modernity, enshrined in institutions of freedom, that allows the modern to represent not just a particular moment in history, inevitably overtaken by the post-modern of a later date, but a uniquely valid form of civilization, valid in the special sense of not falling prey to the problems of legitimacy that afflict any practices that claim authority on the basis of privileged foundations.

Traditionalist opponents of modernity can certainly cling to their fundamentalisms, especially when self-professed modern regimes fail to realize freedom in all its proprietary, moral, household, social, and political dimensions. So long, however, as the traditionalists' opposition to modernity rests upon an appeal to given sacred or profane authority, they cannot overcome the arbitrariness of their own norms, norms that define pre-modernity to the degree that modern institutions emerge through the overthrow of foundational tradition.

Post-modernists, on the other hand, recognize the futility of absolutizing any particular foundations, but they assume that no values and no knowledge claims can be advanced without depending upon some privileged vocabulary or other. On this assumption, modernity's claim to enjoy universal validity and freedom from the given is bogus, concealing some ground reflecting a particular heritage or group whose advance of universal norms can only be a play for power, imposing its own values upon all. In this vein, the affirmation of modernity is unmasked as an affirmation of Western particularity, where "what is universalism to the West is imperialism to the rest."[3] This post-modern challenge to the legitimacy of modernity has one basic difficulty. If all normative claims are foundational, leaving reason and conduct incapable of self-determination, that is, free of determination by prior grounds, the truth of this very situation can never be authoritatively established. Post-modernists must either know with an autonomy they deny or admit that their claims are as ideological, as conditioned by arbitrary foundations, as any others. Post-modernism may give ideological support to the fascist challenge to modern institutions of freedom by unmasking rational autonomy as will to power, which can be consistently affirmed only by repudiating all universal rights and imposing the will of one's group without veiling its particularity and arbitrariness. Yet since this enterprise cannot coherently establish any authority for its own deconstruction of rationality or for its

---

3   Samuel P. Huntington, *The Clash of Civilizations and the Remaking of the World Order* (New York: Simon and Schuster Paperbacks, 2003), p. 184.

promotion of a consistent will to power, post-modernism cannot refute the project of modernity.

Although modernity may enjoy special normativity, the traditional, modern, and post-modern alternatives represent the abiding, unmixed options that a civilization can take with regard to foundations: that is, it can remain traditional, privileging a particular set of given practices, it can be modern, embracing institutions of freedom, or it can be post-modern, advancing a particular form of life with brazen recognition of its own perspectival, arbitrary character. Accordingly, once all three forms of civilization have made their appearance, it is possible to speak of an "end" of history in the restricted sense that history may offer repetitions and hybrid combinations of these options, but no fundamentally novel forms of community.

This holds true even if one acknowledges the lingering presence of culturally defined "civilizational" divides that lead theorists such as Samuel Huntington to speak of distinct Western, Latin American, African, Islamic, Sinic, Hindu, Eastern Orthodox, Buddhist, and Japanese civilizations.[4] Each of these "civilizations" can relate to its own cultural heritage in either a pre-modern, modern, or post-modern way, just as each such "civilization" can be torn by conflicts among "intra-civilizational" advocates of these three competing ways of regarding one's cultural ancestry. Needless to say, which of these options prevails has fateful consequences for the significance and legitimacy accorded these cultural differences. Nations of the same cultural heritage may rather align with one another so long as they treat that heritage as a privileged foundation, but once nations recognize the normativity of modernity and its institutions of freedom, cultural differences can no longer retain the same public importance, either domestically or internationally.

How given cultural unities get modified through pre-modern, modern, and post-modern configuration hinges upon two important consequences of the universality of modernity, consequences that fundamentally determine where post-colonial society fits in such a scheme.

The Dual Character of Emergent Modernity

First, because modernity's institutions of freedom do not depend upon any particular culture for their legitimacy, they are inherently capable

---

4   See Huntington, *The Clash of Civilizations and the Remaking of World Order*, pp. 45–8.

of global, not to mention inter-galactic realization. By contrast, because pre-modern civilizations are distinguished by appeal to some particular heritage as their defining basis, they cannot consistently break with their parochial roots and achieve cosmopolitan hegemony. Admittedly, a pre-modern civilization rooted in a missionary religious tradition may strive for world domination so as to impose its faith upon all and create a world-embracing sacred empire. Nevertheless, this exercise of a will to power is contingent upon the successful conversion or extermination of all "infidels". Consequently, the missionary religious empire does not enjoy the universality gained by being indifferent to all given tradition. Rather, whatever global mastery it achieves depends upon the elimination of all cultural others, allowing its particularity to become exclusive. Achieving solitary particularity is not equivalent to attaining genuine universality. Moreover, the global mastery of a particular missionary creed is always in jeopardy from the recurrence of religious diversity, leaving its empire of faith subject to subversion by its own appeal to exclusive religious identity. Because modernity is fundamentally indifferent to religious affiliation and religions are all capable of reforming themselves to conform to the privatization of faith endemic to civil society and self-government, modernity can become global without undermining itself through its own principles.

Nonetheless, nothing in the structure of modernity's institutions of freedom requires, guarantees, or even makes possible that they come into being universally at once. Rather, the supplanting of traditional forms of life by the different spheres of modern community is bound to occur originally in some particular locality marked by some particular heritage. Because the pre-modern is essentially rooted in a given tradition of limited extent, modernization cannot help but proceed in a regional, rather than global context. Moreover, wherever modernity originates, its distinct freedoms can only emerge in a series of developments fostering some of the institutions of freedom before other types come into being. The impossibility of simultaneous birth is due to the structural relation of the different modes of freedom. Self-government may preside over all other forms of freedom, upholding and regulating their integration within the body politic. Yet no political act can freely create property relations, moral autonomy, freedom in the family, or a civil society. This is precluded because citizens cannot engage in self-government unless they already count as property owners, moral agents, and equal partners in marriage, while enjoying equal economic opportunity and legal rights.⁵ A deficit in any of these autonomies undercuts the equal political opportunity of citizens. This is why genuine political democracy need not be externally constrained to safeguard the pre-political rights of citizens. On the contrary, self-government cannot actualize itself unless citizens already enjoy their pre-political autonomy in family and society, whereas true democracy cannot sustain itself unless the state continues to uphold these pre-political spheres of freedom. Elections may be held without enforcement of pre-political rights, but what results will be a bogus democracy (be it "illiberal", "bourgeois", or "sexist") failing to realize equal political opportunity. Accordingly, the genesis of political emancipation must be preceded by all the domestic, social, and cultural developments that make possible household and social emancipation. Because the time and geographical extension of these developments are prey to all the vagaries of historical accident, any instantaneous or uniform formation is precluded. The final release from feudalism may, as Marx observes, at one blow disengage kinship from commerce and rule, while separating social position from political power.⁶ Nevertheless, the revolution that baptizes a free family, a civil society, and a republic will still present the universal rights of modernity in a regional debut.

Taken together, the universality of modernity and the regionality of the birth of the modern render the globalization of modernity something more complicated than merely a transformation of the pre-modern into the modern.

To begin with, the advent of modern institutions in a particular region creates a divide between two forms of pre-modernity. One pre-modernity stands distinguished as the womb of original revolution—that is, as that pre-modern civilization that transforms itself into the modern. The metamorphosis of this pre-modernity has a pathway defined by what must occur for the institutions of freedom to arise. The requirements of this original genesis of the modern is of course dictated by the structures of

---

5 This is why Hegel is correct to remark that a constitution cannot be produced through an act of making, as Napoleon learned in trying to impose a modern constitution upon Spain. A constitution can only become more than a piece of paper if the non-political prerequisites of political freedom are already at hand. Because non-political spheres are not directly administered by the state, they cannot be brought into being by political action alone. See G.W.F. Hegel, *Elements of the Philosophy of Right*, trans. H.B. Nisbet (Cambridge: Cambridge University Press, 1991), addition to paragraph 274, pp. 312–13.

6 Marx makes this point in *On the Jewish Question*. See Karl Marx, *Early Writings*, trans. T.B. Bottomore (New York: McGraw Hill, 1964), pp. 29–30.

freedom and the reformations of culture that make it compatible with the exercise of rights. Accordingly, the conception of this genesis is posterior to the conception of the institutions of right, which is why Hegel in the *Philosophy of Right* is correct to analyze the history of the emergence of freedom[7] only after having conceived property right, morality, family, civil society, state, and international relations. Nonetheless, even if the genesis of the modern must include specific transformations, this requirement does not dictate that the historical emergence of modernity is itself necessary.

Hegel, of course, has often been alleged to treat the history of freedom, that is, the genesis of modernity, as a necessary process. Significantly, however, his lectures on the philosophy of history begin with the empirical *hypothesis* that institutions of freedom have in large part arisen in our day, a hypothesis which then enables us to interpret history up to the present as a history of the emergence of freedom.[8] Moreover, in analyzing that history, the different way stations do not comprise successive transformations of the same community. Rather, Hegel gives us more of a transmigration of soul, where the development of freedom leaps from one nation to another, albeit within the general orbit of the West, before a modernity arises that can spread its wings beyond a particular people and make itself a global civilization. If each successive form necessarily generated the next stage, one would expect a metamorphosis of one and the same people. That this is not the case suggests that although the original genesis of modernity may have a form dictated by its conclusion, the arrival at that destination rests upon much that is contingent.

Even if this is so, once modern institutions first arise within a particular region, all other communities stand in a new situation. Some may manage, at least temporarily, to close themselves off from contact with the first modern society and then autonomously metamorphose into a modern society in their own right (as Japan may have done). Others may alternately linger in their own isolated pre-modernity. Wherever such seclusion is overcome, however, pre-modern societies become subject to a modernization from without. Since the original modern society has a regional identity, the modernization it may foist on other pre-modern societies will take on the appearance of a regional assimilation, even if it involves the establishment of universally valid institutions.

---

7 Hegel, *Elements of the Philosophy of Right*, paragraphs 341–60, pp. 372–80.

8 G.W.F. Hegel, *The Philosophy of History*, trans. J. Sibree (New York: Dover Publications, 1956), p. 9.

In terrestrial terms, where the original modern society has arisen in the West, external modernization will appear in some respect as a process of Westernization.

Whether "Westernization" and "modernization" completely converge depends upon several factors. If the transformations in question simply entail establishing purely universal structures of freedom, "Westernization" will be identical with modernization from without. If, alternately, the transformations involve imposing practices specific to Western culture in its contingent particularity, "Westernization" becomes a particular form of modernization that may well diverge from the modernization that an isolated non-Western community may autonomously achieve. When, for example, Atatürk imposes fashions of modern Western dress as compulsory features of his program to modernize Turkey, he conflates culturally relative conventions with the universal normative institutions of freedom truly distinguishing modernity. The same mistake is made by anti-Western fundamentalists who regard men's wearing of Western clothes to be modern, but women's wearing of them to be Westernization,[9] and by apologists of Asian Tiger autocracy, who decry democratization as Westernization, not modernization. Because the emancipation of women and representative democracy are both obligatory to the equal opportunities of modernity, they cannot be Western but not modern.

That there is any discrepancy between Westernization and modernization presumes, of course, that what distinguish Western civilization are not cultural features uniquely enabling a community to modernize itself autonomously. If non-Western culture did lack such features, as Hegel, Marx, and Weber all suggest, then the only way non-Western civilization could be modernized would be under the aegis of an external Westernization. In that case, a rigid divide would separate the pre-modernity that transformed itself into Western modernity and the pre-modernity of non-Western civilization.

The Globalizing Tendencies of Emergent Modernity

Whether or not a pre-modern community is able to modernize itself, the whole question of an external modernization remains irrepressible due to

---

9   See Bernard Lewis, *What Went Wrong? Western Impact and Middle Eastern Response* (New York: Oxford University Press, 2002), p. 76.

the globalizing tendencies of any emergent modernity.[10] These globalizing tendencies have two parallel dimensions, one rooted in the structure of civil society, the other following from the exclusive normativity of self-determination.

Although civil society comprises an ethical community whose members interact in function of the pursuit of particular self-selected ends, their association is universal in scope, reaching as far as market interdependence, legal recognition, and economic welfare considerations extend. Political community may erect frontiers separating different states, but civil relations transcend all such borders. This is why economic, legal, and other civil rights warrant international guarantee under the rubric of "human rights", applying equally to non-citizens and citizens, in contrast to national rights to political participation.[11] It is also why states must take special measures to prevent national sovereignty from being undermined by transnational social developments, such as the growth of multinational enterprise and multinational financial and regulatory integration (for example the European Union). Moreover, as Hegel early observed,[12] and Marx and Rosa Luxemburg[13] would later stress, the commodity relations of civil society drive it beyond itself to penetrate pre-modern societies in search of an expanding market furnishing new consumers, new sources of raw materials and manufacture, and new pools of labor. With civil society endowing individuals with the freedom to determine their needs and occupation under the social condition of enabling others to do the same, the resulting market demand engenders a multiplication and refinement of needs and production, liberating the accumulation of wealth of any natural limits.[14] The resulting pressures of competition make an enterprise's survival depend upon increasing sales and profits and the investment these make possible. To the degree that competitive success cannot always be achieved by increasing market share at the expense of

---

10   For if modern community inherently possesses a globalizing dynamic, any pre-modern community is liable to suffer that external impact, irrespective of its own internal metamorphic potential.

11   For this reason, recent United States' legislation depriving resident aliens of welfare benefits is contrary to the rights of civil society.

12   Hegel, *Elements of the Philosophy of Right*, paragraphs 245, 246, 248, pp. 267–8, 269.

13   Rosa Luxemburg, *The Accumulation of Capital*, trans. Agnes Schwarzschild (New York: Monthly Review Press, 1968), p. 329 ff.

14   Hegel spells out the basic logic of these developments in paragraphs 190–95 of his analysis of the "System of Needs" in the *Philosophy of Right*.

other firms or by maintaining market share in a growing internal market, the expansion of civil society's market into other regions becomes an imperative of its own economic dynamic.

How this break through occurs is colored by modernity's general normative tendencies to globalization. On its own self-understanding, the modern community must regard all pre-modern formations as oppressive regimes violating the rights that only institutions of freedom can actualize. Even though traditional communities must command sufficient consent to maintain their own authority and may well be enthusiastically supported by the overwhelming majority of their members, voluntary conformity to tradition is not equivalent to self-determination. This discrepancy between preference and freedom is most obvious in the case of popular dictators, such as, at certain points in their catastrophic careers, Hitler or Stalin. They may have the consent of the majority, but they cannot provide the participation in self-government that political self-determination requires. The same deficit applies to the voluntary acceptance of family arrangements ruled by traditional hierarchies or of social orders organized by hereditary rank. Without the institutions of free households and civil society, individuals cannot enjoy their family and social rights even if they experience domestic and social happiness. To consistently hold itself to the foundation-free standard of freedom, modernity must regard right as uniquely universally valid and not as a parochial heritage, in the manner of Rawlsian advocates of "reflective equilibrium", communitarian particularists, and post-modern fascists. But then modernity cannot consistently celebrate the diversity of pre-modern civilization. Modernity must instead regard global modernization as a normative imperative.[15]

This imperative would apply to pre-modern civilizations whether or not they have the capability for an internal, autonomous modernization. If a contemporaneous traditional community lacked the inner resources

---

15   This is not equivalent to making *Westernization* a global imperative, or for that matter, consolidating Western domination of the world, as Huntington suggests (see Huntington, *The Clash of Civilizations and the Remaking of World Order*, p. 92). Even if modernity first arises in the West, global modernization need not involve Westernization. The universal structures of modern freedom can just as well be given an Eastern as a Western veneer of contingent non-conflicting cultural clothing. Indeed, as Huntington admits (although confusing modernity with normatively neutral technological progress), "the world is becoming more modern and less Western" (Huntington, *The Clash of Civiliziations and the Remaking of World Order*, p. 78).

to revolutionize itself, then the modern community would face the burden of engineering that transformation from without. If, alternately, a traditional community had the ability to modernize itself, the coexisting modern community would still face the challenge of facilitating that metamorphosis with whatever external aid is possible.

These imperatives of global modernization assume that self-determination can be externally imposed, or, more specifically, that modernization can be forced upon pre-modern civilization without corrupting the desired establishment of right. Yet can communities be compelled to be free? It is tempting to answer this question by drawing an analogy between making another individual autonomous and making another community self-determined. Kant formulates the general problem in his "Doctrine of Virtue" by arguing that individuals cannot make others autonomous, for example moral, but can only promote their happiness by helping secure the satisfaction of their desires.[16] Kant's argument might appear to apply uniquely to moral autonomy since moral self-determination revolves around choosing to act with the right purposes and intentions, an internal matter that external intervention can hardly control. By contrast, the other freedoms exercised in property, family, economic, legal, and political relations have an external dimension that can be affected from without. After all, if determining oneself as an owner, a spouse and parent, a market agent, a legal subject, and a citizen depends upon recognition by others and common exercise of the freedoms comprising the different institutions of right, self-determination will depend upon the contributions of other agents. Nevertheless, Kant argues that colonial or imperial domination of another people is unjust no matter what norms the latter obey and no matter what the liberating intentions of their new masters.[17] Since Kant models right after the self-legislation of moral autonomy, any external imposition of institutions will automatically lack that self-legislating character, even if the new order establishes the putative structures of freedom.

Yet might the absence of self-legislation in the *establishment* of the institutions of freedom be endemic to the process of modernization, whether that process be internal or external in origin? Self-legislation as an institutional engagement is specific to democratic self-government.

---

16 Immanuel Kant, *The Metaphysics of Morals*, trans. Mary Gregor (New York: Cambridge University Press, 1991), p. 191.

17 Kant, *The Metaphysics of Morals*, paragraphs 58 and 62, pp. 154–5 and 158–9.

Spouses and parents may codetermine household management, but the scope of the family is a particular right and welfare to which legislation cannot be restricted.[18] Although market activity may conform to economic law, economic agents do not consciously enact the rules of competition. Only self-government involves a freedom with the universal reach requiring rule by law. Nevertheless, as a structure of ethical community, political democracy can itself only operate on the basis of an existing constitution, whose own establishment is not an act of self-government, but rather the result of a founding process involving a plurality of antecedent developments. The emergence of self-government depends upon the formation of pre-political institutions,[19] including the universal recognition of property rights (and the abolition of slavery), the acceptance of moral autonomy (and the religious reformation it requires), the rise of civil society's market economy (and the overthrow of feudal bondage), the institution of civil courts and due process, and the formation of public welfare agencies to guarantee equal economic opportunity. Only with these pre-political transformations can any founding of a democratic constitution signify more than the charade that "people's democracies" once represented. Since these enabling pre-political developments are no more pre-ordained than is political revolution, actual constitution making is a contingent affair of history, fundamentally different from self-legislation.[20] This is true whether the constitution making be an internal affair or a product of external modernization.

Either way, the interconnection of pre-political and political freedom indicates that modernization requires a preponderant engagement of individuals in each of the practices in which right has its exercise. Moreover, because these practices are modes of self-determination, modern institutions cannot be imposed from without unless the recipients are willing to break with their interrupted tradition and interact in terms of their received rights. Although such willingness cannot be reduced to self-legislation, it has its own internal dimension.

---

18   Although Hegel undercuts the freedom of spouses by admitting a traditional hierarchy between husband and wife, he recognizes that the ethical community of the family is particular in scope. See Hegel, *The Philosophy of Right*, paragraphs 161–72.

19   Hegel emphasizes this in the remarks to paragraphs 273 and 274, and the addition to paragraph 274 of his *Elements of the Philosophy of Right*, pp. 311–13.

20   Hegel points this out in the addition to paragraph 274 of his *Elements of the Philosophy of Right*, p. 313.

Accordingly, it makes little sense to follow the Kantian/Rousseauian gambit of judging internal and external modernizations by whether they result from self-legislation. A more plausible strategy consists in first conceiving how the structure of the different institutions of freedom determines the possible interactions between an original modernity and the pre-modern communities it confronts. Once these possibilities are identified, a better judgment can be made of the ethical problems of external modernization and of the colonial and post-colonial predicaments it engenders.

Modernity and the Logic of Colonialism

To understand colonialism and its post-colonial aftermath in relation to modernization, one must think through how the two globalizing tendencies of modernity work themselves out once a modern society has arisen in a particular locality. Since the modern norms that call into question pre-modern communities equally preside over how the emergent modern society interacts with its pre-modern counterparts, it makes sense first to examine how the globalizing dynamic of civil society impacts upon pre-modernity and then to investigate how the principles of modern freedom apply to the resulting situation.

What then are the salient features that push civil society beyond itself, setting the stage for colonial and imperialist expansion? The market enables individuals to pursue particular ends of their own choosing as a right. The market does so by providing the institution within which individual interrelate solely in function of self-selected needs for commodities, choosing both what to acquire and what to offer in exchange. Although each market participant can only achieve its particular end by seeking what others have chosen to offer in return for providing them what they choose to need, the resulting interdependence comprises the condition under which individuals exercise the right to choose their occupation and their needs in reciprocity with others. The market thereby liberates individuals from being assigned roles in production and consumption on the basis of factors such as hereditary rank, gender, and ethnicity, which are privileged by tradition independently of individual choice. By effecting this liberation, the market multiplies and endlessly differentiates needs, means of satisfaction, and the forms of earning, since what alone limits exchange are not fixed traditions or natural necessity, but the arbitrary concatenated choices of individuals. This conventional explosion in the variety of market need and marketed goods engenders demand for commodities that lie beyond the market's own boundaries. At the same time, the arbitrariness of market relations entails a predicament where demand may just as well fall short of supply, leaving civil society too poor to sustain independently the ever expanding pursuit of wealth to which enterprises must aim in order to sustain the investments required to achieve the production and marketing advantages necessitated by competition.[21]

This confronts civil society with complementary alternatives to realize the economic freedom of its members. On the one hand, if civil society cannot adequately reduce unemployment through internal public interventions such as public works or subsidized incentives for employers, it must export its own unemployable labor. On the other hand, if sufficient internal market growth cannot be sustained by credit expansion and deficit spending, civil society must draw upon new supply and demand for which the only remaining source is the abiding pre-modern civilizations that have still escaped modernization.[22]

These parallel injunctions might seem achievable by means of the basic modality of civil association: commodity exchange. Although pre-modern society limits civil freedom by traditional divisions that organize household, economic, and legal relations by factors given independently of the self-determination of individuals, commodity exchange can still conceivably play a circumscribed role within the interstices of traditional community. After all, pre-modern societies may contain markets operating besides predominating non-market distributions of work and goods. Trade between pre-modern and modern society is therefore possible, as the history of early European penetration of the non-Western world can testify. Unemployed settlers can find earning opportunities in the markets of pre-modern society, just as modern enterprises can obtain labor power, raw materials, and finished goods in exchange for whatever commodities

---

21   Hegel, *Elements of the Philosophy of Right*, paragraphs 190–92, 241–5, pp. 228–9, 265–7.

22   In arguing for the inevitable turn to pre-modern markets and the inevitable collapse of capitalism when they have all been assimilated within the relations of capital, Rosa Luxemburg ignores the internal resources that public works, credit expansion, and deficit spending provide for capital accumulation. This is due to her reliance upon Marx's labor theory of value and the derivative reproduction schemes of capital developed by Marx in volume II of *Capital*, both of which preclude these and other facilitators of economic growth. See Richard Dien Winfield, *The Just Economy* (London: Routledge, 1988), pp. 205–10 for a more detailed critique of Luxemburg's argument.

(including money) traditional communities are willing to obtain in return. Yet can such possibilities satisfy the economic dynamic of civil society, or, for that matter, enable a traditional community to modernize through the purely economic expansion of market relations within its borders?

What frustrates either of these prospects is the fundamental disparity between the limits pre-modern tradition places upon economic freedom and the unlimited pursuit of wealth that an unshackled market generates. Merchants and workshops in pre-modern society may earn through exchange with a fully developed civil society. Nevertheless, their own level of trade and production is inevitably constrained by the traditional arrangements that impose fixed limits upon the needs and occupations of themselves and their compatriots, subordinating their own commerce within a wider scheme of social reproduction from which commodity relations are excluded. Because of such traditional limits upon what can be freely bought and sold, market activity is not only constrained in ways that threaten the competitiveness of indigenous industry, but incapable of autonomously assimilating the economic relations that are regulated by non-market pre-modern relations.

The consequences of this limitation are prefigured in the genesis of the original civil society. Marx documents the key factor in his analysis of the "primitive accumulation of capital",[23] expressly contradicting the base-superstructure economic determinism that would enfeeble Marxism. Namely, the only way that market relations can expand their reach in pre-modern society is through a political intervention that forcibly uproots future wage laborers from the conditions of their traditional sustenance and compels them to seek their living in the market. Otherwise, whatever wealth has been already accumulated through trade and usury will be unable to find continually expanding opportunities for investment and fail to precipitate a transformation of the economy into a system producing goods for exchange and the realization of profit.

What applies to the genesis of the first civil society extends with a special twist to external modernization. Primitive accumulation occurs through annihilation of the traditional livelihoods of people by political actions of their own rulers. Lifting the barriers to market penetration in other pre-modern societies from without can only occur through an imperial domination where the government of an emergent modern society uses its state power to force a pre-modern community to "open"

---

23   Karl Marx, *Capital – Volume I*, trans. Samuel Moore and Edward Aveling (New York: International Publishers, 1967), p. 713 ff.

itself to the globalization of the market. This "opening" cannot consist simply in allowing foreign goods to be imported for purchase. Any such trade concessions still leave intact the pre-modern social formations that exclude commodity relations. Instead, those traditional arrangements must be uprooted by political means. The globalization of civil society through external modernization will thus require an external political intervention, enlisting intrigue and military force to overcome indigenous resistance. As the example of China indicates from the Opium Wars through the adventures of the Comintern, such intervention can retain local rulers but force them to adopt policies overturning traditional social relations or enlist revolutionary movements inspired by modern ideologies to replace traditional leaders with more accommodating native "progressives". Alternately, as the examples of the Americas, Africa, India, Southeast Asia, and Australia all testify, direct imperial rule can dispense with indigenous sovereignty in either of two basic ways. A civil society's own underemployed can be settled on conquered territory in colonies exporting the metropolitan society while banishing surviving traditional communities to unwanted enclaves still subject to metropolitan rule. Alternately, indigenous leadership can be replaced with a colonial administration directly governing the conquered society in accord with the conquerors' interests.

Any of these forms of imperial domination can serve the economic needs that push civil society beyond itself. Yet in so doing, each form gives rise to something distinctly different from the modern society that autonomously arises from within a pre-modern setting. And in each case, the new predicament challenges modernity's normative tendencies to globalization with all too familiar legitimation problems.

Settler colonies present two normative challenges. Although the settlers may reproduce a civil society in which property rights, moral accountability, family freedom, economic opportunity, and legal equality are all upheld, so long as they remain subject to the rule of the metropole, their right to self-government is violated. That right counts, of course, only so long as political freedom is duly regarded as an end in itself rather than as a means to guaranteeing the pre-political civil rights of individuals, as social contract theory would have us believe. In the latter case, benevolent and appreciated colonial rule can satisfy the liberal criteria of protecting person and property with the consent of the governed. If, however, the settlers are to enjoy the full breadth of modernity's embrace of freedom, which liberalism is incapable of completely legitimating, either of two options must be followed: the colony must be transformed into a province of the metropolitan nation, with the same political participation as any other, or the colony must become an independent democracy. Any other halfway house, such as Puerto Rico's "commonwealth" status, violates modernity's norms for political right. Of course, because democracy is an ethical community that sustains itself only insofar as its members participate in self-government, the alternate options of integration into the metropole or independence can only provide a real solution if the settler population predominantly embraces one or the other.

A problem still remains even if national integration or independence gives a willing populace political freedom, at least so long as the indigenous population once banished to reservations has either chosen not or not been permitted to assimilate into the surrounding colonial society. If reservation life simply comprised an ethnic enclave in which the modern rights of property, morality, and family, civil and political freedom were exercised as in any other neighborhood or district, independence or integration would already resolve all abiding normative tensions. Indigenous citizens would enjoy the same civil right accorded all to privately exercise their cultural heritage, provided they do so without trampling on the freedoms of their own members or people from other heritages. If instead the indigenous community follows traditional arrangements at odds with right and/or remains governed by an external authority (for example a Bureau of Indian Affairs), a consistent realization of modern principles of right becomes problematic. Any external authority that lords over indigenous affairs deprives its subjects of the freedoms it usurps. Yet that external rule may well reflect the unwillingness of the reservation population to give up their traditional community and assimilate themselves into the surrounding civil society and democracy that has been imposed upon them. Of course, the encompassing modern society must, to be consistent with its own principles of right, eliminate any barriers to such assimilation. Can, however, the encompassing modern society consistently retain rule over reservations in which tradition trumps right or consistently give complete independence to traditional communities in which modern freedoms are ignored, albeit with the consent of the members?[24]

---

24   These issues call into question the role of the American Revolution as a model for anti-imperialist emancipation. As Bernard Lewis observes, because the American Revolution was made by British settlers, not Native American nationalists, Arab critics of the American model can claim that it represents a triumph of colonialism, where colonists have so completely implanted the metropole's civilization that the mother country need no longer be relied upon to

The latter question dovetails with the central dilemma arising when an autonomously emergent modern regime forces commercial concessions from a pre-modern nation or advances beyond such intrusions to conquer the resisting nation and impose direct colonial rule. In both of these cases, the modern intruder might regard itself as the bearer of the principles of civil society if it moved beyond the rape and plunder of the indigenous society (of which Marx accuses the British in the early expansion of the East India Company[25]) to the introduction and enforcement of universal property relations (including outlawing slavery, serfdom, and other forms of bondage), the recognition of moral autonomy (enforcing a separation of religion and state and religious toleration), the transformation of family relations in accord with principles of equality and codetermination, the enactment of freedom of occupation and public welfare guarantees, and the institution of a legal code and court system in which due process is respected. If these measures are not undertaken, the colonial power can hardly justify its usurpations other than on grounds of a national interest that turns a blind eye to the rights of others. Yet, even if the colonial power moves beyond plunder to forced modernization, the very externality of its intervention raises problems.

These problems are two-fold. First, even if it be granted that the rights of civil society (including property, moral, and household right) are unconditionally valid, their very reality as modes of self-determination depends upon a preponderance of voluntary conformity by entitled individuals. This prevailing rectitude need not involve ideological acceptance, personal happiness, or any other specific psychological attitude. It does, however, require that individuals interact more in recognition and respect than in disregard of the appropriate rights of one another. Consequently, if the external imposition of civil society is to succeed, it must somehow achieve that degree of internal recognition on which its freedoms depend. This, of course, presumes that the individuals involved are themselves acknowledged to be competent to exercise civil rights.

---

subdue the original inhabitants. This critique ignores, however, the normativity of the resulting independent nation, as well as what its own principles prescribe for consistently just treatment of the indigenous population. See Bernard Lewis, *The Crisis of Islam Holy War and Unholy Terror* (New York: Random House, 2004), p. 87.

25   Karl Marx, *Karl Marx on Colonialism and Modernization*, ed. Shlomo Avineri (New York: Anchor Books, 1968), pp. 77–82, 84, 99.

Can the latter acknowledgment be squared, however, with the deprivation of self-government that colonial rule incorporates? Admittedly, the pre-modern nation can hardly be said to afford its members self-rule if traditional governance is at odds with democracy. Yet colonialism's violation of the formal independence of the colonized equally fails to replace traditional tyranny with political autonomy. Arendt has observed that colonial regimes characteristically exercise an external bureaucratic management of their colonial subjects and succeed in doing so only by drawing a racial divide between the indigenous peoples and their metropolitan masters.[26] If the colonial rulers cannot ascribe racial inferiority to their subjects, how can they justify a domination that otherwise violates modern political right? Yet, as much as racism in colonial practice may pave the way for the introduction of racism into the internal political affairs of modern apartheid and fascist regimes, racism can hardly be consistently upheld by any regime that legitimates itself under the banner of modernization and development.

John Stuart Mill argued for a less inconsistent justification of colonialism: namely, that the subject peoples were not racially incapable of governing themselves, but that they first had to undergo a tutelage weaning them from their oppressive cultural traditions before they would be able to participate in the institutions of freedom. Colonialism was therefore a temporary way station, superintending an external modernization that would culminate in independence once the formative process was over.[27] Hegel anticipates this view by arguing in paragraphs 350 and 351 of *Philosophy of Right* that the same unconditioned normativity of freedom that gives heroes the right to found states gives more civilized (for example more modern, free) states the right to regard the mores of traditional communities as inferior and to treat their independence as "merely formal",[28] implicitly sanctioning an external modernization through imperialism. If Hegel's basic insight be granted that political freedom cannot operate without the prior formation of a civil society, including universal property rights, recognition of moral autonomy, the triumph of freedom and equality among spouses in the household, the achievement of equal economic opportunity, and

---

26   Hannah Arendt, *The Origins of Totalitarianism* (New York: Harcourt Brace Jovanovich, 1973), p. 185 ff.

27   See John Stuart Mill, *Considerations on Representative Government*, Chapter XVIII, in John Stuart Mill, *Three Essays* (Oxford: Oxford University Press, 1987), pp. 408–23.

28   Hegel, *Elements of the Philosophy of Right*, p. 376.

the institution of civil law, Mill's and his converging arguments would have some merit, provided two conditions could be met. First, colonial rule would have to be capable of externally fostering these developments without succumbing to a self-serving exploitation of the colony's wealth, and secondly, colonialism would then have to eliminate itself as soon as possible in a transition to independent post-colonial regimes.

To object that such a transformation violates the political freedom of the colonial people has a certain formality if the only alternative were a process whereby a pre-modern regime exercises its own non-democratic rule to modernize its society in preparation for metamorphosing into constitutional self-government. Without national independence, a subject community cannot possibly enjoy the political freedom that provides the capstone to modernity. Yet national independence alone may neither involve self-government nor a free society or household. External and indigenous rulers would both have to eliminate their respective forms of political domination if political emancipation is to succeed. The modernizing initiatives of an indigenous ruler would have no automatic privilege unless two principles hold true. First, it must be the case that only an internal modernization can engender the level of voluntary cooperation required for the operation of the institutions of freedom. But if those institutions abstract from affiliation to tradition, why should adhesion to them depend upon the ancestry of the modernizers, especially if traditional rulers owe their authority to mores at odds with emancipation? Secondly, it must be true that external modernization can never resist the temptations of colonial exploitations. Yet are colonial and imperial regimes immune from self-critique, internal political struggles, and external pressures that can all lead them to refrain from international rape and pillage? Although the situations are somewhat distinct, the examples of post-war Japan and West Germany suggest that external rulers can expeditiously eliminate the remnants of pre- and post-modern tyranny and reconstruct modern family, social, and political institutions of freedom with widespread popular support.

In any case, the genesis of the institutions of freedom can never conform to their actuality. Conformity is impossible because the volition founding constitutional democracy can never be an exercise of constitutional self-government. For this reason, neither route to independence can strictly accord with right any more than can the primitive accumulation helping form the first civil society. Since what is at stake in each case is realizing a good that is not yet at hand, the situation is one of moral accountability rather than ethical responsibility, where one is bound by duties already realized in the association to which one belongs. The prescribed task may consist clearly enough in contributing to the rise of universal property right, moral autonomy, household emancipation, civil society, and democratic self-government. Yet because the rights and duties contained in this result cannot be fully applicable until it is attained, their standard provides no unequivocal guidelines for what means to their implementation are genuinely necessary, let alone permissible.

Can the same predicament be said to apply to the post-colonial nation that a consistently modern colonizer must finally decolonize?

Principles of the Post-Colonial Predicament

In distinction from independent settler colonies, a post-colonial nation carries the burden of three decisive features.

First, it contains the vestiges of pre-modern traditions, not isolated in reservations, but spread throughout society under the scaffold of a modern constitution mandating in varying degrees the upholding of property, moral, family, social, and political self-determination. These pre-modern vestiges can involve tribalism or caste hierarchies that undercut the universal solidarity of citizenship, privilege hereditary elders at the expense of self-government and social freedom, and impose a patriarchy at home and in public that deprives women of their rights and deprives the nation of their social and political contributions. Alternately, religious traditions may resist secular freedoms by retaining abject forms of nature worship or sacred laws conflicting with the civil legal enforcement of property, household, and social rights, inhibiting the full development of commercial relations and self-government. In all these ways, the indigenous pre-modern culture continues to hamper the "development" by which modern emancipation can proceed.

Second, post-colonial nations carry the burden of the deformations in household, social, and political life created by the exploitation of colonial masters. This may involve the despoliation of the natural resources of the post-colonial nation, the destruction of its traditional economy, and the enfeeblement of its own industrialization in deference to the economic interests of the imperial metropole. These difficulties will be compounded by the resulting damage to family bonds under the onslaught of mass pauperization and the neglect of indigenous educational, social, and political infrastructures. The newly independent post-colonial nations will then be left sorely bereft of sufficient trained bureaucrats, teachers, doctors, and other professionals, not to mention a labor force with the health, literacy, and vocational training needed for competitive economic growth.

Finally, the post-colonial nation's emergent civil society bears the burdens of competing economically, culturally, and militarily with established modern states. These "developed" nations enjoy the benefit of a longer, more matured formation of capital, giving them a crushing advantage in international economic competition. With an accumulation of wealth far outstripping that of post-colonial nations, the autonomously modernized countries have much greater scientific and technological resources, as well as the military advantages all this provides. To the extent that the established modern societies are duly civil, they further make greater use of their human capital, by extending educational and vocational opportunities with least restriction, while providing the social welfare guarantees that insure general access to health care, child care, and decent housing. Moreover, the "developed" nations escape the internal handicaps posed by the persistence of pre-modern traditions as well as the deformations created by the exploitation of colonial masters.

The resulting discrepancy in economic, cultural, and military influence between "developed" and "underdeveloped" post-colonial nations has led some post-colonial theorists to regard the coming of independence to be a purely formal transition. On this view, colonial rule is supplanted by a neo-colonial domination changing the national identity of the local administrators but otherwise leaving the post-colonial masses in the same plight, suffering with decimated traditions, chronic pauperization, and overwhelmed civil institutions struggling with corruption and bankruptcy. If Marx were right that capital dominates civil society and that civil society subordinates the state, independence would mean little more than this empty formality. The preponderant advantage of foreign capital would allow it to still control the decolonized society and utilize its newly independent government as no less a lackey for foreign exploitation than the defunct colonial administration.

The situation is very different, however, if 1) social interest groups, civil law, and public welfare agencies can uphold the economic opportunity of all, and 2) the state can be preeminent over civil society, not only by legislating and enforcing the laws that uphold pre-political freedom, but by regulating civil society to prevent social inequality from translating itself into political privilege and by thwarting foreign economic interests from dominating domestic society and politics. If the state can protect itself from domestic and foreign social domination, while insuring that social oppression is restricted and democratic freedom maintained, post-colonial political independence can have a double significance. First, provided independence involves not just formal liberty from foreign domination, but the concrete freedom of political self-determination, it represents the culminating phase of modernization, adding the final structure of freedom that pre-modern community has lacked: constitutional democracy. Second, it offers the post-colonial nation all the opportunities that political intervention provides for restricting the influence of foreign and domestic interests upon the development of its own society and political life.

The richest and most competitive nations may promote a free trade ideology to roll back all such political intervention, but every independent state retains the option of regulating its own economy and its relation to foreign capital. Uncompensated nationalizations, tariff and import quotas, limits on foreign ownership of enterprises, flaunting patent and copyright agreements, and other subsidies for domestic commerce all have certain costs, but political independence alone makes it possible to wager these risks. This is true even if newly independent regimes fail to develop genuine self-government and revert to autocratic rule that serves the interest of oligarchs rather than citizens at large.

The history of colonial liberation reflects the new opportunities that political independence provides. Although independence movements have followed various ideologies, they have generally embraced modern ideals of social and political justice, diverging primarily by giving different interpretations of what institutions are required to realize freedom. Whether inspired by Jefferson or Marx, the makers of independence have made themselves vehicles of modernization, bringing modern political relations (and their deformities) to their nation, rather than resuscitating traditional rulers and their communities. Indeed, the very appeal to nationalism has involved the introduction of a very non-traditional community uniting individuals in terms not of pre-modern hierarchies, but the equality of citizenship in a nation of one's own.

Further, each independent nation has attempted to use its own political regulation over society and commerce to orient its development away from the self-serving policies of past colonial masters. This may not be an easy task, but that it can be entertained at all suggests that the supremacy of state over civil society is not just a Hegelian dream.

Still, the endemic disadvantages of newly independent post-colonial regimes do make them vulnerable to foreign economic and cultural domination, as well as to domestic tyrannies, debilitating oppression at home and in society, pervasive corruption,[29] and strife between pre-modern groupings.

---

29   This may comprise the same corruption that self-modernized nations contend with, where money earned in the market is used to influence power.

Whatever the current conjuncture, the future of post-colonial development is no more predetermined than the fate of freedom in the nations that first autonomously modernized. The inequalities between developed and underdeveloped, North and South may intensify, undermining the ability of post-colonial institutions to realize the freedoms they still might promise. Fundamentalist and tribal reaction may succeed in tearing down the incomplete constructions of civil society and political democracy, just as a resurgent fascism may threaten the "developed" nations that fail to fulfill the family, social, and political liberation that modernity has put before us. These options will remain possibilities not just on earth in the twenty-first century, but wherever in the universe intelligent life may emerge and whatever be the particular narratives of its religious traditions. In every case, whatever the future brings, the challenges of autonomous and external modernization will surface anew once the timeless normativity of freedom is rediscovered.

Whether modernity marches on to a consistent global realization, whether traditional reaction or post-modern counterrevolution rejuvenates the rule of foundations, whether natural or human catastrophes banish intelligent life from the planet, and whether these same options play themselves out in other galaxies are contingent matters whose indeterminacy is guaranteed by the freedom of the future from the past. Yet the contingency of the triumph of modernity is no blemish on the legitimacy of the modern project. Precisely because self-determination depends on no foundations, the normativity of freedom always retains authority, forever extending validity to modernity, forever emancipating the future of truth, right, beauty, and faith from the hold of the past, and forever enabling the truth of the past to be free of interests in the future.

Islam and the Post-Colonial Predicament

These general prospects of autonomous and external modernization frame the world-historical context within which Islamist Jihad presents its challenge to the project of modernity. That challenge can be comprehended only by examining the specific nature of Islam and how it impinges

---

Given the increased likelihood of unaccountable bureaucracy and autocracy under post-colonial conditions, corruption there will likely also involve the kind where those who hold power use it to enrich themselves. Lewis describes the latter as distinctive of corruption in the Muslim Middle East. See Lewis, *What Went Wrong?*, p. 63.

on the process of modernization, both as an obstacle to autonomous modernization and as a basis for an anti-modern revolt springing from the post-colonial condition.

Chapter 5

Islam and Modernity

The Liberating Promise of Islam

In important respects, Islam comprises a religious faith that has overcome many of the doctrinal obstacles to modernization. Like Judaism and Christianity before it, Islam has purged the divine of all residual traces of natural determination at odds with rational agency. Allah is the Lord, a pure, absolute will in which divinity has been thoroughly spiritualized, divested of physical encumberment and the finitude any such shaping entails. Like Jehovah, Allah is the creator, existing entirely independently of nature, which is relegated to a creation generated by and remaining over and against the divine. Although this renders humanity itself a creation, Allah, like Jehovah and the God of Christianity, has created humanity in the image of the divine, a divine whose characterization as the sovereign Lord implies that the essence of humanity resides in freedom of will. Insofar as freedom of will is universal to competent agents, the prescriptions of Islam essentially apply to all its faithful, irrespective of rank. Accordingly, the commands of Islam take the form of religious law, extending equally to everyone under divine jurisdiction. In this respect, Islam follows in the footsteps of the Torah's Ten Commandments, which broke new ground by putting all Jews under the same rules, in contrast to the separate particular codes of hierarchical caste communities.

Yet, whereas Jewish religious law applies without discrimination to all Jews, Islam extends this universality beyond the limits of a particular people, joining Christianity in the ranks of religions that proselytize, offering a way of relating to the divine that is inherently good for all. This extended universality overcomes the given boundary of consanguinity, which has no right to put any frontiers on relations of freedom. Admittedly, the restriction of Jewish religious law to a particular people is not based on any natural privileging. Not only does the Torah proclaim that all humanity is created in the image of God, but the relation between the Jewish people and the divine is based on a freely entered covenant, rather than upon a bond determined by nature, independently of will.[1] Nevertheless, Islam's claim to be a universal religion, prescribing a relation to Allah to which all should subscribe, seems most congruent with the global normativity of modernity's civilization of freedom.

Secondly, the basic observances of Islam pose no inherent obstacle to the exercise of rights. The primary Muslim injunctions to follow certain dietary restrictions, periodically fast, perform ritual washings, pray towards Mecca five times daily, make a pilgrimage to Mecca, and give to charity need not violate any entitled freedoms of others, provided these injunctions apply only to those who have voluntarily adhered to the faith. Making these observances compulsory would violate personal liberties, including moral rights of conscience and civil rights of religious freedom. If, however, these injunctions hold only for those who freely subscribe to the faith, then all can be followed without transgressing the privatization of religion that modernity mandates. Of course, charity can count as an ethical injunction, abetting the right to equal economic opportunity, provided the charity is distributed to all the needy and not just to Muslims,[2] and provided it does not turn into an extortion of wealth for other purposes, such as religious indoctrination or terrorism. So too, the further Muslim injunction to defend the faith can serve freedom when religious rights are jeopardized and the defense of Islam does not suppress the religious freedoms of others, as in illiberal Muslim countries that criminalize apostasy and blasphemy and ban proselytizing by and public worship of other faiths. Still, as Kant points out,[3] ritual dietary restrictions, ablutions, daily prayers, and pilgrimages have no intrinsic ethical value or any necessary connection to the practice of religious faith in general. Like all ceremonial observances, they have a purely conventional character, whose spiritual significance would hardly be altered if instead of five times daily, prayers were offered twice, pilgrimage were made to somewhere other than Mecca, or mutton were proscribed instead

---

1   Moreover, Jehovah's covenant with Noah (Genesis 9:1–17) implicitly extends to all humanity.

2   Whether historically existing Muslim charities have observed this proviso is questionable, especially given the *jizya*, or poll tax, traditionally exacted from *dhimmis*, members of non Muslim non-pagan communities accorded second-class status under Islamic imperial rule.

3   See Immanuel Kant, *Religion Within the Limits of Reason Alone*, trans. Theodore M. Greene and Hoyt H. Hudson (New York: Harper & Row, 1960), p. 182.

of pork.[4] Nonetheless, such rituals no more conflict with the rights of their practitioners or of others than do the corresponding observances of Jews or Sikhs.

Thirdly, Islam does not privilege any clerical body with exclusive rights to interpret the faith and mediate believers' relation to the divine. Instead, the very distinction between an official clerical hierarchy and a religiously subordinate laity is largely absent, for all believers are regarded as capable of accepting faith and receiving Muhammad's message of revelation on their own. Islamic religious scholars may issue *fatwahs* comprising judgments applying holy law. Nonetheless, no central religious authority ordains which scholars' judgments command unequivocal official respect, or precludes any other self-proclaimed religious judges from tendering *fatwahs* of their own. Accordingly, no reformation to dethrone a clerical hierarchy is needed to open the door to the freedom of conscience, where each individual can exercise the moral freedom of determining the good.[5]

On all these counts, Islam has offered a faith open to all, in which converts can find an equality and solidarity unmatched by the religious traditions that sanctified nature and natural differences, or left the life of spirit subordinate to an infallible clerical hierarchy. Admittedly, Muslim equality signifies equal subjection to a common discipline as a loyal member of the community of Islam,[6] and not equal participation in self-government, a civil society in which slavery and gender inequalities are

---

4   This capricious character of ritual is reflected in Spinoza's observation that the ceremonial observances of the Torah are good only by convention and accordingly hold out the promise of merely material gain, rather than the true salvation awaiting those who follow the moral commands of the Decalogue. See Chapter 5 of his *Theological-Political Treatise* in Spinoza, *The Complete Works*, trans. Samuel Shirley, ed. Michael L. Morgan (Indianapolis: Hackett Publishing Company, 2002), pp. 435–6.

5   The absence of any separate ecclesiastical law and authority is also grounded in the Caliphate unification of religious and political authority, which not only precludes a distinct clerical establishment, but also non-clerical lawyers, who might administer law without being *ulema*, doctors of holy law. As Lewis points out, lawyers emerged in the Islamic world only under the impact of the modernized West. See Bernard Lewis, *What Went Wrong? Western Impact and Middle Eastern Response* (New York: Oxford University Press, 2002), p. 53.

6   George Anastaplo points this out in *But Not Philosophy* (Lanham, MD: Lexington Books, 2002), p. 189.

eliminated, or an emancipated household.[7] Nevertheless, by providing a faith to which all are welcome and under which all are ruled by the same laws of a divine implicitly affirming the absolute supremacy of free will, Islam has offered the promise of liberation from the bondage to which contemporaneous religions contributed by sanctioning subjection to natural powers, caste privilege, or priestly despotism.[8]

The Life of Muhammad and the Specter of the Caliphate

Nonetheless, the universality of Islamic faith becomes of utmost danger to modern institutions of freedom when it gets informed by hegemonic aspirations enshrined in the religious significance given the life of Muhammad in Islamic tradition, not only in the Koran but also in the Hadith, whose traditions depict his sayings and practice. Unlike the prophets of the Jews, Muhammad does not lead a particular people out of oppression to establish a community of its own where it can enter into a true relation to the divine. Instead, Muhammad is a religious conqueror, forging an ever widening empire of faith by military conquest and imperial rule.

Muhammad begins his career in Mecca, professing to have been visited by the angel Gabriel with divine revelations enjoining him to spread the message of one god, creator of nature and humanity, offering salvation to all who turn away from idolatry and accept the universal solidarity of obedience to the same revealed law commanded by Allah. Hounded out of Mecca by the local rulers, whose religious tradition he challenges, Muhammad flees to Medina, leaving behind reliance upon prophetic persuasion.

Unlike other prophets who never do more than devote themselves to preaching and effecting voluntary conversion to the faith, Muhammad now assumes leadership of a rebel force, which takes local control of Medina, fends off attacks from Mecca, and finally sets out to conquer that

---

7   Muslim legal and religious equality does not traditionally apply to unbelievers, slaves, and women. As Lewis observes, this leaves women worst off, for although slaves can be freed by their master and unbelievers can always choose to convert and obtain equality, Muslim tradition dooms women to an irremediable inferiority. See Lewis, *What Went Wrong?*, pp. 67–8.

8   As late as the early nineteenth century, Lewis claims, a *man* of humble origins had more opportunity to attain wealth, power, and dignity in Islamic territories than anywhere in Christian Europe, including the French republic. See Lewis, *What Went Wrong?*, pp. 83–4.

idolatrous Arab city. Successful in his military campaign, Muhammad now invests himself as the ruler of a united Arabia, combining supreme political authority with the highest religious authority, reigning as the exclusive prophet of God.

In this capacity, Muhammad lays down the laws of Allah as revealed to him, sits in judgment over their application, and enforces their commands. All spheres of life in the new Muslim state are subject to the divine law Muhammad transmits and in whose name he rules. Whereas in imperial Rome the Emperor was worshipped as God, Muhammad and his Caliph successors are the vice-regent of the sovereign, Allah.[9] Muhammad and the caliphs do not head an ecclesiastical hierarchy with its own laws and institutions, operating in parallel with the state they rule. Unlike Christendom, where clergy contrasts with laity and distinguishable religious and political authorities may cooperate or conflict, Islamic religious authority is one and the same as political authority. Whereas Christian canon law differentiates itself from civil law, the revealed holy law that governs Muhammad's Islamic state is the one and only legality that presides with obligatory sanction over all human affairs.[10]

As subjects of the new regime of Allah, pagan idolators face choosing between conversion to Islam with full equality as Muslims or enslavement or death.[11] Jews and Christians who spurn conversion are either banished or relegated to a second-class existence, subject to a special poll tax (*jizya*)[12]

---

9   Lewis gives these apt formulations in *What Went Wrong?*, p. 97.

10   For this reason, as Lewis observes, Muslim men of religion are traditionally not clergy in any professional sense. Not until modernizing developments begin separating religion from government can one speak of a professional Muslim clergy and clerical institutions, as found first in the waning Ottoman Empire and today in Iran, where, as Lewis observes, the emergence of councils of ayatollahs and equivalents of an inquisition may provoke a reformation, challenging the privileged authority of the new Muslim clerical establishment. See Lewis, *What Went Wrong?*, pp. 98–100, 108–9.

11   As Lewis observes, polytheist idolators would be tolerated when Islamic conquerors confronted absorbing the immensity of Hindu India. See Lewis, *What Went Wrong?*, p. 114.

12   As Lewis points out, the *jizya* is mandated in the Koran (9:29): "Fight against those who do not believe in God or in the last day, who do not forbid what God and His Apostle have declared forbidden, who do not practice the religion of truth, though they be the People of the Book until they pay the jizya, directly and humbly." See *the Crisis of Islam*, pp. 45–6.

and various restrictions upon their occupation and religious activities.[13] The world is now divided into two realms, the *Dar al Islam*, the realm of Islam, that in which God rules through the divine law administered by Muhammad and his Caliph successors, and the *Dar al Harb*, the realm of war, the world that spurns the sovereignty of God and which it is religiously imperative to bring under divine law. Through Muhammad's founding example, the stage is set for holy war to pass from defense to offense, an offense without limit, given the universal reach of Islamic proselytization.

In contrast, the particularism of Judaism becomes its saving grace. Because Judaism, like Hinduism, has no aspirations of proselytization, religious empire is never sought. The only occasions when rule and religious identity become connected are in exceptional circumstances, such as enslavement under the Pharaohs and the Nazi final solution, when the political independence of the religious community may be necessary to secure the safety of the faithful and the continued practice of the religion.

Admittedly, when Moses leads the Jews out of Egypt, Jehovah has no mercy for the Canaanites who dwell in the land promised to be given over to Jewish settlement.[14] The brutal extermination of the Canaanites and the self-separation of the Jews from all other peoples may, as Kant observes, draw down upon them the charge of misanthropy.[15] Yet, even though Jehovah has Moses (at least on Moses' own account)[16] order the massacre of the Jews who revert to idolatry,[17] once the Exodus is

---

13   These restrictions imposed upon *dhimmis* have traditionally included the wearing of distinctive clothing and the distinctive marking of their domiciles, as well as prohibitions of riding horses or bearing arms, of openly performing rites of worship or customs that would scandalize Muslims, of building edifices higher than Muslims' or new places of worship, and of bearing witness against a Muslim. See Joseph Schacht, and C.E. Bosworth, *The Legacy of Islam* (Oxford: Oxford University Press, 1964), pp. 130–32.

14   Jehovah commands: "Thou shalt utterly destroy them." See Deuteronomy 20:17–18.

15   Immanuel Kant, *Religion Within the Limits of Reason Alone*, note, p. 172.

16   Walzer points out that God's command remains hearsay, raising the issue of whether this first revolutionary purge was Moses' own "Machiavellian" initiative. See Michael Walzer, *Exodus and Revolution* (New York: Basic Books, 1985), pp. 56–61. In any event, given that the purge follows the covenant between the Jews and God, Walzer can claim that its ultimate justification lies in the popular willingness by which they have committed themselves to the commandments of God. See Walzer, *Exodus and Revolution*, pp. 74–5.

17   Exodus 32:26–8.

completed, the Jews can follow their own law without being intolerant of their surrounding neighbors.[18]

Significantly, when the Jews establish their own nation, political power is not invested in religious authority. The people who Moses leads out of captivity in Egypt all individually consent to follow divine law in return for "milk and honey" and a society in which the security of all will insure that no one can oppress others like the Pharaoh they have fled. That divine law consists in moral commandments and religious observances that can all be fulfilled privately without conflicting with civil law and toleration of other ecumenical faiths. Nothing in the Ten Commandments precludes further legislation by independent political authorities. Neither Moses nor his descendants become kings, nor is political authority wielded by the Levites who become a tribe of priests. When kingship is finally established under David and Solomon, the new monarchs do not possess any special religious position.

Hence, it can come as no surprise that when the Nazi Holocaust leads to the founding of a new state of Israel, the Jewish identity of the body politic has more to do with guarantees of free Jewish immigration than with religious rule. Otherwise, Judaism is generally fit for the privatization of faith allowing integration into civil society. Toleration of other faiths poses no threat to Jewish religious practice, so long as these faiths are tolerant in return. By the same token, Jewish religious law can consistently apply solely to the Jewish community. Since that law prescribes communal observances that by and large leave secular freedoms unimpeached, it readily allows for a secular law governing citizens of all faiths in an emancipated body politic. Admittedly, Orthodox Judaism may spurn interfaith marriage and personal freedom of belief. Yet even these impositions on marital and moral freedom can coexist with civil society so long as they persist as self-imposed commitments in a freely joined ghetto.

By contrast, the imperial tradition of Muhammadan conquest transforms the universality of Islamic dogma into a global challenge to moral accountability, family rights, civil society, and self-government. Other pre-modern opponents to modernization defend traditions rooted in a particular heritage that cannot consistently seek to transgress its local bounds and strive for world supremacy. They may seek to roll back the external modernizations

---

18 As Exodus 23:9 commands: "Thou shalt not oppress a stranger: for ye know the heart of a stranger, seeing ye were strangers in the land of Egypt." Walzer cites this in reference to the dilemma posed by the 1967 Israeli victory that made Israel ruler over occupied lands. See Walzer, *Exodus and Revolution*, p. 140.

already implanted within their community and screen out any further development, but this resistance, such as waged by Hindu militancy, has no global ambition. By contrast, because Islam has sufficiently spiritualized the divine so that Allah appeals to all humanity, the example of Muhammad the religious conqueror has no regional limitation.

The only limitations that the Muhammadan example faces are the contingent bounds of faith. Whereas the modern institutions of freedom are indifferent to religious belief, the Islamic empire of faith can only achieve global hegemony if all infidels choose to convert or if Islamic zealots compel them to do so or exterminate them. This is why the universal appeal of Islam retains a particularity that distinguishes its global spread from the universality of modernity, which can encompass all duly privatized religions and cultural formations.

For this reason, the abstract character of Muslim devotion becomes the progenitor of a world-embracing fanaticism. With the disembodied, purified will of the one Lord the absolute object of a devotion that grants no worldly differences any independent significance, Muslim fervor strives to surmount all frontiers in an all-inclusive empire of faith, in which no pre-existing conventions have any intrinsic value. As Hegel observes, the essence of fanaticism lies in an enthusiasm for something abstract, against which everything concrete stands as a limit to be obliterated.[19] During the French Revolution, the secular fanatics, Robespierre and the Jacobins, held to an abstract conception of freedom, for which all difference between the will of all and the general will of the state was intolerable, where all political divisions and institutional hierarchy represented a limitation upon autonomy and the identity of ruler and ruled. Consequently, their advance of abstract freedom entailed a destructive terror, extinguishing all dissidence and pluralism. Similarly, the abstract enthusiasm fueling the pursuit of a world empire of faith makes religion a vehicle of terror, sweeping aside all dissenting cultural forms it finds in its wake. Whereas Robespierre's principle was "*liberté et la terreur*", so the principle of Islamic world conquest can be seen to be "*la religion et la terreur*".[20]

Admittedly, only in the centuries immediately following Muhammad did the Caliphate unite the entire *Dar al Islam* under one state with one ruler combining the highest political and religious authority. Yet, with the splintering of the Muslim world into separate dynasties, the Caliphate

---

19 G.W.F. Hegel, *The Philosophy of History*, trans. J. Sibree (New York: Dover Publications, 1956), p. 358.

20 Hegel, *The Philosophy of History*, p. 358.

ideal still persisted. On the one hand, the Caliphate hung on to life until 1924, when Turkey, under Mustafa Kemal's leadership, abolished the position, after having two years earlier abolished the Sultanate with which it had been combined.[21] The Caliph may no longer have retained political leadership of all Muslim lands, but until 1922 he did rule over at least one of the major dynasties (from Baghdad during the Abbasid reign and finally, from Istanbul during the Ottoman Empire) while laying claim to religious leadership of all Muslims. Moreover, in each coexisting dynasty *Shariah* law still ruled supreme,[22] albeit administered by different emirs, all recognizing the spiritual authority of the Caliph. On the other hand, the dream of a single united Muslim polity lived on,[23] both as a rallying cry in the wars for supremacy between the different Muslim dynasties and as inspiration for further world conquest.

The all-inclusive reach of the Caliphate might seem tarnished by the Arab preeminence reflected in the retention of the *Hijaz*, containing Mecca and Medina, as the center of pilgrimage and in the spread of Arabic as the language of Islam.[24] Certainly, contemporary Islamist militancy, bankrolled by Saudi Arabian Wahhabi interests, has increasingly supplanted the local forms of prevailing Muslim culture with an Arabic liturgy and specifically Arabic architectural and artistic motifs,[25] just as earlier, the conquering Caliphs destroyed much of the pre-Islamic cultural

---

21 See Bernard Lewis, *The Crisis of Islam: Holy War and Unholy Terror* (New York: Random House, 2004), p. xvii.

22 A notable, but shortlived exception to this hegemonic supremacy was the rule of the Mogul emperor Akbar (1556–1605), who abolished the *jizya*, accepted the right of Hindus to proselytize or reconvert, permitted Hindus to build new temples, allowed Hindu wives of Muslims to keep their faith, patronized Hindu arts and sciences, affirmed reason as the basis for approaching religion, and generally supported freedom of worship. See Aziz Ahmad, *Studies in Islamic Culture in the Indian Environment* (New Delhi: Oxford University Press, 1964), pp. 80, 86, 88, 167–81.

23 See Lewis, *The Crisis of Islam*, p. xxi.

24 Mustafa Kemal, in a civics manual he dictated to his daughter, writes that "The religion founded by Muhammad was based on a policy of setting Arab nationalism above all other nationalisms." See Andrew Mango, *Atatürk: The Biography of the Founder of Modern Turkey* (Woodstock and New York: The Overlook Press, 2002), p. 469.

25 For a discussion of this Arab cultural imperialism, see V.S. Naipaul, *Beyond Belief: Islamic Excursions Among the Converted Peoples* (New York: Vintage International, 1998), p. xi.

traditions, both physically and in the public imagination. Nevertheless, this Arabic cultural imperialism could just as well be jettisoned, while retaining political sovereignty for Allah through retention of the supreme reign of *Shariah*. The Koran could be worshipped in local languages in mosques of a completely local architecture without subverting the hegemonic aspirations of a world-embracing Islam, aspirations which have no ultimate stake in any particular ethnic heritage.

These aspirations are reflected in the recurring Islamist demands to make Islamic law supreme and exclusive, to liquidate any cultural dissidence that questions the authority of Islam, to destroy non-Muslim culture, both contemporary and historical, and to ban proselytization by other religions. These demands apply wherever Muslims reside, just as support for conversion to Islam remains a global imperative.

The resonance of these demands in wider Islamic practice is hard to ignore. Symptomatic of the combination of universal inclusion and hegemonic exclusivity is the operation of the holy sites in Mecca and Medina, to which converts from all over the world are welcomed, but from which non-Muslims have been strictly barred ever since their expulsion by the Caliph 'Umar in 641 CE.[26] Similarly, whereas Muslim tradition fosters mutual toleration among competing schools of *Shariah* jurisprudence,[27] following the Hadith saying attributed to Muhammad that "Difference of opinion within my community is a (sign of divine) mercy," apostasy is regarded as an intolerable offense punishable by death.[28] The same unwillingness to privatize Islam, practice ecumenical toleration,[29] and allow public space to have any secular independence is

---

26 As Lewis explains, the Caliph 'Umar ordered this expulsion of the resident Jews and Christians to fulfill the Prophet's deathbed injunction, "Let there not be two religions in Arabia." See Bernard Lewis, *The Crisis of Islam*, p. xxix.

27 As Lewis observes, the absence of any separate ecclesiastical institutions in traditional Islam precludes any official distinguishing between orthodoxy and heresy in the manner of Christian ecclesiastic authority. Hence, divisions within Islam, such as that opposing Sunnis and Shias, arose over disputes not about religious doctrine but about political leadership. See Lewis, *What Went Wrong?*, p. 100. See Edward Gibbon for a similar analysis of why Islam has not been prey to the same degree of doctrinal controversies as Christianity – *The Decline and Fall of the Roman Empire: Volume III* (New York: Heritage Press, 1946), p. 1779.

28 See Lewis, *The Crisis of Islam*, p. 41, and Ibn Warraq, *Why I Am Not A Muslim* (Amherst, NY: Prometheus Books, 1995), p. 241.

29 Lewis points out that in the Ottoman Empire, each religious community was permitted free practice of its religion to a degree unmatched in Christian

manifest by how calls for prayer are broadcast so invasively as to allow no escape from their interference, by how the five times daily prayers get conducted in public thoroughfares, bringing all other life to a halt, and by how these intrusions have been traditionally accompanied by prohibitions of any public display of religious worship by other faiths, as still today stringently enforced in Saudi Arabia.

So long as adherence to the Muhammadan example ties Islam to the creation of an Islamic state, all modern freedoms, with the possible exception of ownership, stand in jeopardy. Even if Islamic law were interpreted so as to prohibit unequal treatment of women and homosexuals, to substitute incarceration for amputations, brandings, stonings, and other pre-modern corporal punishments,[30] and to forbid holy warriors to kidnap, torture, mutilate, and murder civilians, the mere advocacy of religious rule would still signify a repudiation of the privatization of faith and religious tolerance, undercutting the freedom of conscience, marital and parental rights, the social autonomy of civil society, and self-government. Under the religious law of an Islamic regime, individuals lose the right to determine independently the moral good, forfeit their entitlement to marry and raise children to autonomy without subordination to a particular creed, become deprived of the cultural liberty and legal equality generic to civil society, and have their political freedom usurped by religious authority. The economic development fostered by and prerequisite for the flourishing of civil freedom will be just as stifled as the autonomous development of science, art, theology, and philosophy. Given the exclusive normativity of self-determination, Islamist reaction cannot coherently represent Allah in a manner congruent with the truth of humanity.

Europe. Nonetheless, proselytizing Muslims was still a capital offense, indicative of the official primacy of Islam and the limits of ecumenical toleration. See Bernard Lewis, *What Went Wrong?*, p. 33.

30 These corporal punishments all violate right by striking at the body of the malefactor instead of curtailing the willing against right in which wrong consists. The latter calls for incarceration, whereas the former amounts to treating persons as animals, on whom physical pain is to be inflicted. Only with the recognition of rights in modern times has the maiming, torture, and the expressly grisly public execution of criminals become recognized as inappropriate forms of punishment.

Islam, the Post-Colonial Condition, and Islamist Reaction

Because the Islamist agenda shackles every freedom save, perhaps, for property rights,[31] it should be no surprise that the Caliphate tradition Islamists seek to renew dominated territories failing to modernize themselves. From the Atlantic coast of north Africa to the farthest reaches of the East Indian archipelago, the predominantly Muslim territories offer a spectacle of vastly different peoples subdued by the conquering Islamic empire and then subjected to a post-colonial condition, where modernity first intruded through imperial domination by foreign powers that independently modernized.[32] Whether it be the Russian conquest of the Muslim Caucasus, Transcaucasus, and Central Asian lands, the British takeover of Mogul India, the British and Dutch colonization of the Malaysian and Indonesian Muslim Sultanates, or the British and French conquest of the Arab Middle East and north Africa, the same broad story has repeated itself.[33] Pre-modern Islamic regimes have fallen easy prey to self-modernized nations, whose colonial rule has imposed an external modernization, eventually precipitating its own elimination, both by fostering indigenous independence movements laying claim to modern notions of social and political emancipation and by having to contend with the principled inconsistency of continued colonial domination. With few exceptions,[34] what has resulted are newly independent nations struggling with the common post-colonial liabilities of persisting, but crippled pre-modern traditions, economic and administrative developments

---

31 Even this can be questioned if Islamists uphold the holy laws that tolerate slavery, concubinage, and curtailments of the property rights of non-Muslims and women. Islamists usually refrain from reinstating the Koranic provisions on slavery (Lewis, *What Went Wrong?*, p. 89), but not from reimposing all the other curtailments on persons and their property rights.

32 This holds true even of Muslim nations, such as Turkey, Iran, Saudi Arabia, and Afghanistan, which have largely escaped direct colonial rule, but have still been subject to transforming influences disproportionately originating from without.

33 For a capsule description of the phases of imperial domination, see Lewis, *The Crisis of Islam*, pp. 56–9.

34 The principal exception is the part of the Ottoman Empire that escaped dismemberment by Balkan nationalist movements and colonization by Britain and France and struck out on a belated road of self-modernization as the Republic of Turkey.

deformed by colonial exploitation, and the relative pauperization, undercapitalization, corruption, and instability of the new public order.

What role has Islam played in rendering the Muslim world a decadent empire, slipping far behind the self-modernizing civilization that found it such easy prey to master? It is tempting to locate the source of Muslim stagnation and underdevelopment in such factors as the traditional Islamic prohibition of usury, the failure of Islamic law to recognize corporate legal persons,[35] and the severe restrictions upon women in every public arena. Certainly the ban on usury obstructs the mobilization of wealth for competitive investment, hobbling banking and credit systems, and restricting the accumulation of capital. No nation that refuses to avail itself of the commercial advantages of financial loans can hope to compete against unencumbered economies, or achieve the technological development that markets generate as a necessity of competition and upon which military strength more and more depends. By the same token, the traditional refusal to grant legal status to corporate entities hobbles the development of commercial enterprises as well as the voluntary civil associations that promote economic and social opportunity and self-management at local, regional, and national levels. Similarly, a nation that confines its women to domestic servitude squanders half its human capital, while leaving the upbringing of all to mothers deprived of education and exposure to the public world.[36] How can the *Dar al Islam* hope to stand on a par with countries that fully mobilize the talents of men and women alike?[37] On all these counts, the Islamic world appears to have set itself up as an easy pawn for external domination, once other civilizations break free of their own traditional chains, liberating social and political relations from patriarchal feudal kinship ties, extricating the family from civil society and civil society from the state.

Yet neither Islamic prohibitions of usury, lack of recognition of corporate status, nor curtailments of women's opportunities would be decisive if they were merely voluntarily observed provisos of a freely entered religious community. Then, whatever religious law prescribes

---

35 Lewis, *What Went Wrong?*, p. 111.

36 On the latter points, see Lewis, *What Went Wrong?*, p. 157.

37 Although this may be moot to an Islamist like Ayatollah Khomeini, who insisted on barring women from occupations such as teaching because of inevitably immoral results, it was duly recognized by Atatürk, who argued that Turkey could never catch up with the modern world if only half the population was modernized. See Lewis, *What Went Wrong?*, pp. 72–3.

would be a private matter, with no binding hold on state, society, or household. Regimes would be free to establish a different frame of commerce more amenable to economic development, just as they would be free to enfranchise women, eliminate prohibitions against female employment and independent movement, and impose equality between spouses in the regulation of the family and its property. Similarly, individual households would be at liberty to decide how strictly to follow religious tradition and choose accordingly their own earning activities, including money lending and borrowing, as well as decide how adult members participate in society and politics. What precludes all this is not simply Koranic doctrine, but the Islamic tradition of making religious law compulsory and exclusively supreme, combining religious and political authority, and regarding all governance as the rule of Allah, whose revealed commands provide all the law that need be promulgated. Only because of Caliphate hegemony, where *Shariah* enjoys unchallenged reign and Islam is an all-encompassing "whole way of life", can any traditional Muslim injunctions possess the authority sufficient to stifle the emergence of the emancipated family, a civil society in which freedom of occupation and social interest group advocacy are exercised, and a secular body politic in which citizens exercise self-government, participating in self-legislation through representative democracy.

By accepting law to be exclusively Islamic, rule to be an expression of the sovereignty of Allah, and obedience to be compulsory, the Muslim world casts a pall upon the autonomous development of philosophy,[38] art, theology, and science,[39] strangles any economic activities that violate sacred tradition, precludes any break from religiously sanctioned patriarchy, and bars any political emancipation that introduces the freedom of living under laws that citizens impose upon themselves. This is why the regions dominated by Islam, an Islam defined by the more than thousand year reign of the Caliphate, could not be the arena in which modern relations of freedom first came into existence and flowered. Thanks to its religious tradition, the Muslim world has condemned itself to the pre-modern

---

38   It is thus no surprise that Islamic philosophy is primarily scholastic, accepting without question the authority of the Koran.

39   Although one is tempted to draw parallels between the Inquisition's treatment of European astronomers and the razing of the great observatory at Galata, Istanbul, in 1577 by decree of the Sultan on advice of the Chief Mufti, the continuation of the Caliphate precluded anything comparable to the Renaissance. See Lewis, *What Went Wrong* (pp. 79–81) for a brief survey of this and other examples of the stultification of independent inquiry in the Muslim world.

stagnation that would leave it prey to imperial domination and finally relegate it to a post-colonial malaise.

The Islamist remedy to that condition cannot possibly succeed. The faded glory of the Caliphate cannot be retrieved in a modern world, whose glaring inequalities in power and wealth reflect the very limitations of the Islamist solution. Secular regimes may be overthrown, religious law may be reimposed, commercial borrowing and lending may be proscribed, women may be returned to domestic seclusion, secular education may give way to madrasa indoctrination, and cultural and scientific activity may fall under a fundamentalist veil. None of these developments, however, can reduce the glaring disparity in the accumulation of wealth, technology, scientific research, and military power that fuels the opposition of North and South, of developed and underdeveloped, of erstwhile metropole and post-colonial miasma. Nor can political Islam resolve the accompanying discrepancies in opportunity, health, education, and the other amenities of life that reflect the destruction of traditional forms of security and the incomplete and undercapitalized growth of modern replacements. Muslim charity and Islamist neighborhood welfare organizations can provide some relief to the needy, but neither can remove the enduring obstacles to economic development that the hegemony of holy law imposes. Islamist rule may expel the current elites that preside in autocratic splendor over their pauperized and tyrannized subjects, but religious police cannot replace corrupt inequity with household, social, and political opportunity. Ayatollah Khomeini may proclaim that "Islam is politics or it is nothing,"[40] but Iranian Islamist rule only exemplifies how a return to Islamic theocracy has trapped a new generation of Muslims in further servile obedience and unfulfilled dreams of prosperity and power.

The contrast between the retrograde prospects of Islamist anti-modern reaction and the modernizing outcome of the Puritan "Revolution of the Saints" is telling. At a time when the world of Islam was slipping into decline, Calvin, Cromwell, and other Protestant militants led radical political upheavals that would set the stage for the West to emerge as the first civilization to modernize independently.

In certain respects, Protestant political zealotry shared much in common with the Islamist militancy that followed more than three centuries later. Both movements politically mobilize religion in face of a disintegrating traditional order in which hierarchical status relations, such as patriarchy, clan and tribal community, hereditary rank, and corporate

---

40 Lewis, *The Crisis of Islam*, p. 8.

privilege, have yet to give way to modern impersonal relations of social and political equality. Both movements erupt at a moment of social corruption and disarray, where the weakening of traditional authority has left a widespread "experience of masterlessness"[41], making many long for a new rigid discipline and self-discipline, promising an order founded upon conviction and purpose. Both movements demand a voluntary commitment, where partisans participate in the struggle not due to their given status, but by choosing to be zealous, equal to every other holy warrior, and subject to the same tests and discipline. And in both cases, the zeal and discipline of the new movement forges a community of otherwise unrelated brethren, who can therein find security apart from the decaying systems of tradition.[42]

Yet, in key ways, the Puritan saints are worlds apart from the Islamist Jihadists. The Protestant zealots may want to establish a new order under whose discipline individuals can achieve godliness, but that order does not have a revealed body of sacred law on which its magistrates can depend. Allah may have endowed Muslims with an all-encompassing *Shariah*, preempting self-legislation, but Protestants worship a God encountered in conscience and not in positive edicts of revelation. Hence, Protestants must make their own laws and appeal to their own inner moral tribunal to insure that they serve godliness. To give their law-making authority, they must enter into covenant with one another (for example Calvin's Geneva Covenant of 1537, the Scottish National Covenant, and the Puritan army's Agreement of the People),[43] rather than swear obedience to some putative deputy of God's holy law. On this basis, Puritan revolution asserts the conscientious power of parliament against the King and nobles, setting in motion a political revolution that will empower the self-legislating forces of democracy, as well as the consensual family and civil society underlying the emergence of self-government.[44] By contrast, Islamists remain bound to the political sovereignty of Allah, rendering parliamentary government at best a dispensable strategic interlude. Moreover, whereas the Protestant "Revolution of the Saints" leads to the emergence of modernity, Islamist

---

41 Michael Walzer, *The Revolution of the Saints: A Study in the Origins of Radical Politics* (Cambridge, MA: Harvard University Press, 1982), p. 313.

42 Walzer, *Revolution of the Saints*, pp. 315, 317–19.

43 Walzer, *Exodus and Revolution*, p. 89.

44 Walzer explains that the illiberal parliamentary control of the saints gives way once their new disciplinary order produces sufficient security to make ceaseless saintly zeal appear unnecessary and repressive. See Walzer, *Revolution of the Saints*, pp. 302, 319.

Jihad reacts against a modernization already under way for three centuries. Instead of forwarding emancipation, Islamist reaction presents another obstruction that can only deepen the malaise of the post-colonial condition, a condition in no small way precipitated by the diverging paths of Protestant and Islamic zealotry.

National Revolution and the Modernization of Islam

Because the war against terrorism is a war against Islamist reaction, victory cannot ultimately be achieved without the modernization of Islam. Terrorist groups can be dismantled. Religious political parties can be prohibited and clerics can be banned from holding public office. Quality secular education can be made universally available. Palestinian independence can be won, United States forces can leave the Fertile Crescent and the Gulf, and unprecedented efforts can be made to diminish the glaring inequalities between the nations who modernized themselves and those subject to external modernization. Yet none of these measures will suffice to rid modernity of its greatest pre-modern antagonist unless Islam fully modernizes itself.

Can national revolution lead the remnants of the *Dar al Islam* to a belated modernity without an independent religious reformation?

Mustafa Kemal, the Atatürk, provides the classic answer to this question through the upheaval he led as the greatest secular modernizer the Muslim world has yet produced. As a young military officer and rising nationalist, Kemal, like his other Young Turk compatriots, could hardly take up the mantle of religious reformer and, in the guise of a new Caliph, rescue the Ottoman Empire from collapse.[45] Yet, in conjunction with military campaigns against foreign invaders and a national political emancipation, Kemal carried through a cultural revolution that exhibits both the promise and limitations of secular transformation.

Confronting Ottoman decadence and the specter of foreign domination that its weakness invited, Kemal undertook to establish a new political unity within which the freedoms of modernity could be erected. The Ottoman Empire, like the other Islamic realms it succeeded, had a unity

---

45 When Indian Muslims told a visiting Turkish delegation that Muslims abroad wanted Kemal to become Caliph, rather than abolish the Caliphate, Kemal declared the proposal absurd since foreign Muslims could hardly obey a Caliph when they had their own governments. See Mango, *Atatürk: The Biography of the Founder of Modern Turkey*, p. 407.

that transcended all racial, ethnic, and other differences independent of religious affiliation. Realizing the sovereignty of Allah through the hegemonic rule of *Shariah*, which had jurisdiction over every member of a faith open to all, the Muslim state was no more Turkish than Arab. Instead of combining ethnic and political identity, the Caliphate made religion the defining unity of the realm. It is therefore not surprising that traditional Muslim histories describe the vicissitudes of the Islamic empire but never separate histories of the Arabs, the Persians, the Turks, or any other people.[46] The same resistance to linking national and territorial identity is reflected in the traditional absence of any Arabic word for Arabia and of any Turkish word for Turkey.[47]

If the union of religion and rule must be broken, as a fundamental condition for modernization and the emancipation it promises, what unity can be given to the community freed of Caliphate despotism? In important respects, the answer to this question was already defined by the disintegration of the European bastions of the Ottoman Empire through national liberation movements. These did not define themselves religiously. If they had, what would have been fought for were Christian states, united by adherence to at least the same branch of Christianity (for example Eastern Orthodox, Catholic, and so on), and somehow joining rule and religion. Yet, not only were the Christian sects theologically opposed to combining what is God's with what is Caesar's, but the new nations were founded by movements of ethnic national solidarity, uniting Greeks as Greeks and Slavs as Slavs.[48] Consequently, groups not belonging to the new nation's identifying people had suspect membership and faced the prospect of ethnic cleansing. Accordingly, Kemal confronted a situation where the independence of Greece and the Balkan states was accompanied by transfers of ethnic populations from and into the remaining territories of the splintering Ottoman realm. Although the population transfers were by no means exhaustive, they left the remaining people of the Ottoman Empire primarily defined by two converging unities: Islamic identity and Turkish identity. The latter

---

46   Lewis, *The Crisis of Islam*, xxi., Lewis, *What Went Wrong?*, p. 103.

47   Lewis, *The Crisis of Islam*, xxi.

48   Nevertheless, the Greek, Serbian, and Bulgarian Eastern Orthodox Churches did actively support their respective nationalist movements, not to establish priestly rule, but to establish secular states in which Christians no longer had second-class status because of their religious identity. See Mango, *Atatürk: The Biography of the Founder of Modern Turkey*, p. 9.

ethnicity emerged by default when the British and French succeeded in detaching the Arab territories from the Ottoman Empire, reducing it to the borders of what would now become Turkey.

Ideally speaking, political emancipation is achieved when institutions of self-government afford equal political opportunity to citizens whose right to participate is based not upon sharing a common ethnic identity, but in adhering to a common constitution. When the state is a nation state, conflating citizenship with membership in a historically given ethnic group, the political rights of individuals of other ethnicities stand in jeopardy. Nonetheless, because political emancipation occurs in nations that are ordered by pre-modern identities given by birth, such as ethnicity, self-government not uncommonly arises within borders that largely correspond with the historical territory of an ethnically defined people.

In the case of Turkey, Islamic rule had already supplanted ethnic territoriality with a different pre-modern situation, whose dissolution nevertheless precipitated similar results. In order to replace the Islamic state of the Ottoman Empire with a modern polity, Kemal had to overturn two features antithetic to political freedom: first, the political sovereignty of Allah, secured by the rule of *Shariah* under the Caliphate marriage of political and religious authority, and secondly, the dynastic absolutism of the sultanate, which determined the head of state and religion by birth and gave the Sultan autocratic power. Under pressure to modernize from the encroaching European powers, the Ottoman dynasty was already beginning to cede power to parliamentary institutions[49] when Kemal rose through the ranks of the military, newly trained, equipped, and organized with the help of German officers. Still, two decisive steps had to be taken to complete the break from the petrified confines of the Muslim state. On the one hand, the Sultan had to be made no more than a constitutional monarch, reduced to nominal figurehead of a government freed from dynastic control. On the other hand, the religious position of the Caliph had to be severed from political leadership, so as to free parliament to make

---

49 By 1876, the modernizing reforms collectively known as the *Tanzimat* had culminated in the adoption of an Ottoman constitution and the establishment of constitutional government with a military and civilian bureaucracy, without, however, eliminating the supremacy of either the Sultanate or the Caliphate with which it was combined. See Mango, *Atatürk: The Biography of the Founder of Modern Turkey*, pp. 6–7. Although the new constitution mandated a nominated senate and popularly elected lower chamber, parliament was dismissed in 1878 by the Sultan and would not reconvene until three decades later. See Lewis, *What Went Wrong?*, pp. 58, 60.

its own secular law binding on the body politic, subject to constitutional, rather than clerical review. Then, the Caliph would be the politically powerless highest religious authority of an Islam whose holy law would have relinquished public command. Instead, *Shariah* would be reduced to a privatized religious code voluntarily followed by the faithful, with no right to override conflicting parliamentary law.

Taking these steps has no connection in principle with establishing a nation state, whose unity is tied to a particular ethnicity. Nonetheless, the national liberations of the Greeks and Balkan Slavs, compounded by the accompanying population transfers, and the secession of Arab territories under British and French direction together left the shrunken Ottoman state with a de facto Turkish identity far more homogeneous than ever before.[50] Advancing that ethnic identity had a very pragmatic appeal, for Kemal could much more realistically hope to unite his citizenry around his modernizing project if he appealed to their centuries old ethnic identity[51] rather than to a yet unexperienced identity as a self-governing citizenry. Accordingly, when Kemal undertook to eliminate the despotism of the Sultan, he did so as the Atatürk,[52] the "father of Turkey", leading the National Assembly in 1922 to abolish the Sultanate and replace it with a Turkish Republic. Although the Turkish Grand National Assembly did not thereby establish a republic in which non-Turks were deprived of their rights as citizens, or embrace any Pan-Turkism,[53] the affirmation

---

50 By mid-1922, few Armenians were left and the sizeable Greek population was fast departing. See Mango, *Atatürk: The Biography of the Founder of Modern Turkey*, p. 332.

51 Nonetheless, given the centuries of Caliphate rule, under which Turkish identity was subordinate to Pan-Islamism, it is not surprising that Turkish nationalism first emerged in the urban center of Istanbul, fostered by the impact of Western orientalists who published works about the history of the Turks and their role in the history of Islam, as well as by the agitations of Turkic exiles from the Czarist empire, whose struggle against Russian domination mirrored the nationalist movements of Pan-Slavists in their fight for liberation from Ottoman rule. See Mango, *Atatürk: The Biography of the Founder of Modern Turkey*, p. 96.

52 Mustafa Kemal did not actually take on the surname Atatürk until he gave it to himself in 1934, when the National Assembly made surnames compulsory for Turkish citizens and restricted the surname Atatürk uniquely to Mustafa Kemal. See Mango, *Atatürk: The Biography of the Founder of Modern Turkey*, p. 498.

53 Kemal specifically spoke out against both Pan-Islamism and Pan-Turkism before the National Assembly in 1922. See Mango, *Atatürk: The Biography of*

of the Turkish nation state did involve promoting an ethnically defined national culture under which all citizens would be assimilated, ultimately providing a secular identity challenging that of membership in the *Dar al Islam* or Pan-Islamism. This encouraged affirmation of Turkish as the national language at the expense of any public use or teaching of Greek, Armenian, Kurdish, and the other minority languages. Accordingly, when public secular education was inaugurated, it was conducted exclusively in Turkish.[54] Eventually, notices in foreign languages were prohibited and citizens were encouraged to speak only Turkish in public.[55] The use of non-Turkish ethnic names was officially discouraged by a 1926 Ministry of Education decree.[56] Moreover, a 1934 resettlement law banned entry of people not "attached to Turkish culture", such as gypsies, although a year later, two Greeks, an Armenian, and a Jew were appointed deputies for the first time.[57] It is thus not surprising that accompanying the public pursuit of a Turkish national identity was a readiness to cover over the massive massacres of Armenians perpetrated by the Ottoman Empire during its convulsive death throes.

During the initial groundshaking transformations that saw the Sultanate give way to the Turkish Republic, Atatürk and the Turkish Grand National Assembly did not strike directly at the hegemony of Islam.[58] The new republic still retained Islam as its official religion and kept the office of Caliph, albeit purged of the political power it possessed so long as the Sultanate existed. When Atatürk argued in behalf of abolishing the Sultanate but retaining the Caliphate, he suggested that doing so fit the traditional history of Islam, in which politically impotent Arab Caliphs had wielded religious authority for centuries under the rule of Seljuk Turks in Baghdad and Mamluks in Egypt.[59] Yet, the very fact that the National Assembly made law as an autonomous legislative body meant that the official status of Islam no longer signified the rule of *Shariah*.

---

the Founder of Modern Turkey, p. 332.

54 Mango, *Atatürk: The Biography of the Founder of Modern Turkey*, p. 403.

55 Mango, *Atatürk: The Biography of the Founder of Modern Turkey*, p. 500.

56 Mango, *Atatürk: The Biography of the Founder of Modern Turkey*, p. 428.

57 Mango, *Atatürk: The Biography of the Founder of Modern Turkey*, p. 500.

58 Mustafa Kemal's first proclamation as president of the Grand National Assembly declared, "We, your deputies, swear in the name of God and the Prophet that the claim that we are rebels against the sultan and caliph is a lie. All we want is to save our country from sharing the fate of India and Egypt." See Mango, *Atatürk: The Biography of the Founder of Modern Turkey*, p. 278.

59 Mango, *Atatürk: The Biography of the Founder of Modern Turkey*, p. 363.

This was underscored by the 1923 move of the capital from Istanbul to Ankara, physically separating the government from the Caliph, who now was appointed by the National Assembly and prohibited from wearing any uniform that might imply political or military office.[60] Hence, it was only a matter of time before the Caliph was revealed to be an emperor without clothes and the Turkish Republic revealed itself to be a secular state.

The veil of official Islam was finally removed in a succession of decisive measures, beginning with the abolition of the Caliphate in 1924. That abolition was accompanied by the exiling of all members of the Ottoman dynasty and the abolition of the ministry of canon law and pious foundations, which supervised the rule of *Shariah* over the Ottoman Empire. Islam still remained nominally the official religion, but all Muslim religious institutions were placed under government control, subordinate to the National Assembly, which wielded supreme legislative and executive power, under the guidance of its president, Mustafa Kemal.[61] These measures were shortly followed by the closing down of all religious courts, which applied *Shariah* to personal affairs, such as marriage, divorce, and inheritance.[62] The triumph of civil legality was then secured by adoption of a new secular legal code, modeled on modern Swiss law, complementing the recently enacted constitution of the Turkish Republic.[63] And finally, in 1928, the Assembly completed the disestablishment of Islam by removing the last references to Islam from the constitution and secularizing all oaths of office.[64] To this day, no other Muslim state has followed suit, officially abrogating *Shariah* and purging the constitution of all mention of Islam.[65]

Formally speaking, the separation of religion and rule was a fait accompli with the abolition of the Sultanate and the Caliphate, the subordination of Muslim religious organizations to government control, the replacement of religious courts by civil legality, and the elimination of any public privileging of Islam. Nevertheless, Kemal and his People's Party were fully aware that the completion of a new legal and constitutional

60 Mango, *Atatürk: The Biography of the Founder of Modern Turkey*, pp. 392, 364, 365.

61 Mango, *Atatürk: The Biography of the Founder of Modern Turkey*, p. 404.

62 Mango, *Atatürk: The Biography of the Founder of Modern Turkey*, p. 407.

63 Mango, *Atatürk: The Biography of the Founder of Modern Turkey*, p. 437.

64 Mango, *Atatürk: The Biography of the Founder of Modern Turkey*, p. 463.

65 Lewis, *What Went Wrong?*, p. 106. The multi-faith nation, Lebanon, is the only Middle Eastern state besides Turkey having a written constitution without an established religion. See Lewis, *What Went Wrong?*, p. 108.

framework promulgating the privatization of Islam was not sufficient to realize modern institutions of freedom. What was done in the Assembly in Ankara was one thing, but how citizens continued to live their lives was another. The mere fact that a secular parliamentary government made its laws did not mean that *Shariah* had ceased to govern daily life or that the great mass of the people had ceased believing in Islam being an all-inclusive rule of existence, compromising their allegiance and obedience to the new order.

What was needed was more than a political and legal revolution. The persisting culture of Islam had to be transformed to make it compatible with republican government and civil legality. Yet how can secular political leaders carry off a cultural revolution within a civilization where religion has enjoyed hegemonic public authority?

At times, Mustafa Kemal appealed directly to the faithful, entering mosques to preach sermons in which he argued that Islam's perfection resided in its conformity with truth and reason, a conformity that insures that whatever is rational is true to Islam.[66] He urged mosques to open themselves to discussions of secular affairs and accordingly hold sermons in Turkish addressing contemporary issues.[67] Yet, the sporadic hectoring of a secular outsider could hardly effect theological reformation.

As president of the republic, Kemal would have to achieve a cultural revolution through acts of state. Accordingly, he embarked on a series of measures that sought to mold the daily life of his citizens in accord with the secularizing requirements of modernity.

First, his People's Party, which controlled the Assembly, pushed through bills instituting a unified system of secular public education with instruction in Turkish.[68] This involved closing the madrasas, which gave religious training in Arabic. Now not only were mosques and religious endowments subject to secular regulation, but education was completely removed from religious control and put under government supervision.

In 1929, a year after Arabic numerals were replaced by international numbers, the Arabic script, which never suited Turkish phonetics, was

---

66 Mango, *Atatürk: The Biography of the Founder of Modern Turkey*, pp. 374, 380.

67 Mango, *Atatürk: The Biography of the Founder of Modern Turkey*, p. 374.

68 Mango, *Atatürk: The Biography of the Founder of Modern Turkey*, p. 404.

compulsorily replaced by the Latin alphabet, putting the new generation at a further distance from classical Islam and its Arabic and Persian literatures.[69]

Next, the very flow of time was secularized. Legislation replaced the Muslim era, solar calendar, and system of numbering hours with their modern international counterparts, and Sunday was made the day of rest instead of Friday, the traditional Muslim day for praying in congregation.[70]

A day after the religious courts were abolished, the Muslim prohibition on alcohol was repealed.[71] Further, the government swept aside the *Shariah* ban on human representation by erecting statues of secular heroes, starting with a war monument depicting an arm holding aloft a Turkish flag, followed by a proliferation of pedestals topped by figures of Mustafa Kemal.[72]

Next, traditional dress was subjected to a compulsory modernization. Clerical dress was restricted to clerics recognized by the government and then prohibited from being worn outside of mosques and other venues of religious ceremonies. This effectively made Muslim clerical dress vanish from secular space.[73] Headgear had already undergone modernizing reform under Sultan Mahmut II, who introduced the fez for civil and military officials. Nonetheless, the fez, in contrast to the rimmed European hat, was expressly suited for the prostration of Muslim prayer. Hence, in pursuit of creating a public space that looked as secular as it was intended to be, Mustafa Kemal banished the fez and made the hat compulsory for civil servants.[74] Although not banned, the veiling of women was officially discouraged, while civil service regulations banned headscarves from public premises, including schools.[75]

And, as if to permit Atatürk the last word, upon his death, his body was laid out in state for several days in defiance of the Muslim injunction for quick burial.[76]

---

69 Mango, *Atatürk: The Biography of the Founder of Modern Turkey*, pp. 464–6. Attempts were made to introduce Turkish into the liturgy, but in face of protests, the efforts were kept limited and intermittent. See Mango, *Atatürk: The Biography of the Founder of Modern Turkey*, p. 497.

70 Mango, *Atatürk: The Biography of the Founder of Modern Turkey*, pp. 437, 499.

71 Mango, *Atatürk: The Biography of the Founder of Modern Turkey*, p. 407.

72 Mango, *Atatürk: The Biography of the Founder of Modern Turkey*, p. 411.

73 Mango, *Atatürk: The Biography of the Founder of Modern Turkey*, p. 499.

74 Mango, *Atatürk: The Biography of the Founder of Modern Turkey*, pp. 433, 435.

75 Mango, *Atatürk: The Biography of the Founder of Modern Turkey*, pp. 435.

76 Mango, *Atatürk: The Biography of the Founder of Modern Turkey*, p. 525.

All these measures succeeded in imposing external limits upon organized religious practice and education, as well as blocking the intrusions of Islamic law and ritual in the public domain. As a consequence, it can be said that under the Turkish Republic and its Kemalist cultural revolution, Islam was compelled to be compatible with the external operations of secular society.

Some of those constraints are incompatible with the personal liberties and freedom of religion that modernity's civil society establishes by privatizing faith and providing a public sphere in which individuals can pursue particular interests so long as they facilitate others doing the same. Atatürk's nationalization of Islamic religious institutions involves a public control that goes beyond whatever restrictions are required to insure that a particular religion privately practices its faith without violating the moral and religious freedom of others. So long as religious bodies exercise ecumenical toleration and respect civil legality, they are entitled to govern their own ecclesiastical affairs without direct government supervision. Similarly, access to public secular education may be a right to which all children are entitled, but that does not preclude parents being entitled to give their children religious instruction in private religious schools, so long as that does not interfere with their receiving the secular education they need to enjoy equal opportunity in adult life. Furthermore, although dress should not be tolerated if it interferes with individuals' ability to exercise their rights as full-fledged participants in society and state, religious attire that does not violate such freedoms is a matter of personal liberty and freedom of religion that should not be curtailed. Dress should be a matter of private personal prerogative and civil freedom is violated by Atatürk's prohibition of hooded scarves in public places, including schools, just as it is by the similar prohibitions imposed by the French government today. Admittedly, the adoption of Muslim traditional dress by women may often be not just a personal choice, but an imposition supported by intense family and communal pressure. Moreover, extreme forms of physical covering, such as the burkha, which completely entomb women from head to toe, may not only pose security risks, but prevent women from fully participating in public affairs. Nevertheless, upholding personal freedom of dress, with the proviso that personal costume not interfere with one's opportunities and obligations at home, at work, in court, in sport, in the military, or in politics, is an imperative of right, duly enforceable against those fanatics of tradition who impose codes of dress upon others.

Whether these particular prohibitions be lifted or not, outward conformity by the faithful need not signify inner acceptance. Religion, after all, may involve external observances, but above all, it resides in the inner conviction of belief and pious feeling. So long as faith remains at odds with the secular constraints to which it is confined, those constraints may prove to be as ephemeral as the communist end of history has turned out to be.

The history of Turkey since the death of Atatürk suggests the precarious nature of a secular revolution unaccompanied by a thoroughgoing religious reformation. When one party rule was replaced by multiparty democracy in the 1950s, challenges to Kemalist secularism began to surface. Some of these represent legitimate attempts to rescind the direct government regulations of religious life that curtailed legitimate exercises of religious freedom. In this vein, voluntary religious education was introduced in primary schools, a faculty of theology opened in Ankara, the call to prayer was permitted in Arabic instead of Turkish,[77] and schoolgirls were once again allowed to wear headscarves.[78] Other challenges, however, represent attempts to undermine the separation of religion and politics that Atatürk so strictly maintained. These include measures taken in the 1980s and 1990s by a reconstituted Office of Religious Affairs to publicly finance mosque construction, *require* religious instruction in public schools, and to fund separate Islamic schools.[79] Most ominous has been the resurgence of Islamist public sentiment and the corresponding rise of the Islamist Welfare Party, which won sufficient electoral support in 1995 to take over the government in coalition with other secular parties, under the suspicious eyes of the military, the most adamant bastion of secularism.[80] With the European Union demanding that Turkey rein in the military to satisfy democratic standards for admission, the door may be opening for the Welfare Party to reclaim its old Islamist agenda without compromise.

Although these developments remain of undecided outcome, they present the lesson that national secular revolution must be supplemented by something no political intervention can engineer: religious reformation.

---

77   Mango, *Atatürk: The Biography of the Founder of Modern Turkey*, pp. 530–31.

78   Samuel P. Huntington, *The Clash of Civilizations and the Remaking of World Order* (New York: Simon and Schuster Paperbacks, 2003), p. 147.

79   Huntington, *The Clash of Civilizations and the Remaking of World Order*, p. 147.

80   Huntington, *The Clash of Civilizations and the Remaking of World Order*, p. 148.

Modernization and the Religious Reformation of Islam

Like any other religion, Islam possesses the ability to reinterpret its dogmas to better accord with the autonomies of modernity. The Koran may be held to be the word of Allah and fundamentalists may seek to preclude reformers by privileging a literal reading of the holy text. Yet the Koran cannot interpret itself, or unequivocally sanction a literal reading of itself, or unequivocally indicate what a literal reading actually says.

The Koran may purport to be the word of Allah, but it contains many passages that speak in some other voice, be it that of the Prophet, the angel Gabriel, or some different speaker, just as it contains inconsistencies and grammatical errors that must be explained away.[81] Moreover, as any reader knows, the whole Koran is woefully fragmentary and repetitious,[82] lacking the sustained narrative and coherence exhibited by the Old and New Testaments from which the Koran appears to borrow in fits and starts.[83]

Further, doubts as to whether all or some of Muhammad's pronouncements are really Allah's word cannot be laid to rest by appeal to fulfilled predictions, miracles, or divine interventions. In each provision of substantiating evidence, reports must be introduced whose accuracy and veracity are as questionable as any other historical account.[84]

Nor can reinterpretation be preempted by the doctrine of the infallibility of the consensus (*ijma*) of religious scholars (*ulamas*). Recourse to *ijma* still leaves unanswered which consensus of religious scholars should count. Should authority be vested in the consensus of the Prophet's companions, of his descendants, or of any contemporary group of *ulamas*?[85] And even

---

81 For a catalogue of examples, see Ibn Warraq, *Why I Am Not A Muslim*, pp. 106–15.

82 Gibbon reports that "The word of God and of the apostle was diligently recorded by his disciples on palm-leaves and the shoulder-bones of mutton; and the pages, without order or connexion, were cast into a domestic chest, in the custody of one of his wives. Two years after the death of Mahomet, the sacred volume was collected and published by his friend and successor Abubeker." See Gibbon, *The Decline and Fall of the Roman Empire: Volume III*, p. 1739.

83 One can wonder, as does Anastaplo (*But Not Philosophy*, p. 187), how these features reflect the cultural conditions of Muhammad and his Arab community, but a theological consideration must wonder how the Koran's haphazard organization adequately fits the divine whose word it purports to convey.

84 Anastaplo, *But Not Philosophy*, p. 182.

85 Ibn Warraq raises these issues in *Why I Am Not a Muslim*, p. 166.

if this controversy is decidable, how is the privileged consensus to be understood without further interpretation?

In face of these difficulties, Islam cannot afford to abandon reason in examining its own dogma. The key arguments opening the door to a rational self-reinterpretation of Islam have long been provided by the medieval Islamic philosopher Averroes (Abū al-Walīd Muhammad ibn Ahmad ibn Rushd). In *The Decisive Treatise Determining the Nature of the Connection between Religion and Philosophy*,[86] Averroes (1126–98) argues that the Koran itself invites reason to interpret its text, even though it be the infallible word of God. Not only do several verses of the Koran summon readers to reflect upon its meaning, using intellectual and legal reasoning,[87] but more fundamentally, the very truth of Holy Scripture insures that it cannot conflict with philosophy. Truth cannot oppose truth, whether revealed or proven by rational demonstration.[88] Any attempt to demonstrate otherwise would only uphold the conformity of reason and religious truth, for argumentation to prove that revelation conflicts with reason would be enlisting reason to make its case. Once more, what holds true of revelation would be established by, and therefore correspond to, reason. One can certainly criticize the arguments of philosophers that appear to conflict with revelation. Averroes's predecessor, Algazali (Abū Hāmid Muhammad ibn Muhammad al-Ghazālī, 1058–1111), does just this in *The Incoherence of the Philosophers*, where he attempts to show that the ancient Greek philosophers could not satisfy their own proof conditions when they argued that bodies cannot be resurrected, that God knows universals but not particulars, and that the world is everlasting and not created.[89] However successful such internal criticisms be, they can never preclude philosophers obtaining truth through reason. The failures of

---

86   Professor Ronna Burger, head of Philosophy at Tulane University, New Orleans, has pointed out the importance of this text in conversation.

87   Averroes cites in particular, "Reflect, you have vision" (Koran 59:2). See Averroes, *The Decisive Treatise Determining the Nature of the Connection between Religion and Philosophy*, trans. G.F. Hourani, in *Philosophy in the Middle Ages, Second Edition*, ed. Arthur Hyman and James J. Walsh (Indianapolis: Hackett Publishing, 1986), p. 298.

88   Averroes, *The Decisive Treatise Determining the Nature of the Connection between Religion and Philosophy*, p. 302.

89   Algazali, *Deliverance From Error* and *The Incoherence of the Philosophers*, selections trans. G.F. Hourani, in *Philosophy in the Middle Ages, Second Edition*, ed. Arthur Hyman and James J. Walsh (Indianapolis: Hackett Publishing, 1986), p. 272–3.

particular arguments do not condemn all and any argument, for the futility of philosophy undercuts itself by incoherently using reason to impeach itself. Consequently, as Algazali himself acknowledges,[90] anticipating Averroes,[91] we have due cause to employ the true arguments of philosophers, even those who may not believe in the revelations of the Prophet because they reasoned long before Muhammad received his message (for example Plato and Aristotle) or because they ignore the Koran.

This consideration provides scriptural interpretation with the following guiding rule: whenever the apparent meaning of scripture conflicts with reason, an allegorical interpretation should be found that enables the holy word to exhibit the truth it must possess. Accordingly, it is neither obligatory to take all scripture literally nor to give an allegorical interpretation to every apparent meaning. Rather, interpretation must recognize that scripture has both an apparent and an inner meaning, and then employ reason to unveil the inner meaning when necessary to bring out the truth that must always be presumed to belong to the word of God.[92]

This allows one to understand how the word of God could be revealed in scriptural texts whose apparent meanings contradict one another. As Averroes observes, these discrepancies serve the purpose of summoning rational interpretation to uncover the genuine inner meaning that removes confusion and secures the reasoned truthfulness of religious dogma.[93] Moreover, the very distinction between apparent and inner meaning is no defect in revelation. Rather, as Averroes explains, those who cannot recognize scriptural truth by means of reason can still be led to true belief by the images of literal, apparent meaning, whereas those who follow rational demonstration will be able to secure belief with allegorical interpretations uncovering the ideas that the images of literal meaning suggest.[94]

These arguments provide Islamic reformers with the resources, as well as the theological imperative, to reinterpret the Koran and the other sources of *Shariah* so as to sanitize all the specific rules that, on face value, directly conflict with the rights that reason upholds in establishing the normativity

---

90 Algazali, *Deliverance From Error*, p. 274.

91 Averroes, *The Decisive Treatise Determining the Nature of the Connection between Religion and Philosophy*, p. 299.

92 Averroes, *The Decisive Treatise Determining the Nature of the Connection between Religion and Philosophy*, p. 302.

93 Averroes, *The Decisive Treatise Determining the Nature of the Connection between Religion and Philosophy*, p. 303.

94 Averroes, *The Decisive Treatise Determining the Nature of the Connection between Religion and Philosophy*, pp. 308–9.

of self-determination. This includes the texts that tolerate and regulate slavery (for example suras 4:28, 16:77, 30:28) and concubinage (for example suras 4:3, 23:6, 33:50-52, 70:30),[95] mandate the inferior position of women (for example suras 2:223, 2:228, 4:11-12, 4:34), proscribe homosexuality (for example suras 4:16, 7:80-81), prescribe physical punishments in place of incarceration (for example suras 5:33, 5:38, 24:2-4), make apostasy and blasphemy capital crimes, and discriminate against non-believers, be they pagans or non-Muslim peoples of the Book (for example suras 3:28, 4:141, 5:51, 9:29).[96] Yet, reinterpreting the specific content of *Shariah* to make it compatible with rights cannot call into question the compulsory authority of sacred law, which rests on the political sovereignty of Allah that Caliphate despotism made into a thousand-year Reich and that Islamist reaction dreams of renewing.[97] The modernization of Islam cannot succeed unless it confronts the fundamental impediment to the realization of freedom that lies in this acceptance of the absolute hegemony of religious law. Yet how can Islam consistently relinquish that hegemony without subverting the absolute authority of Allah?

A key part of the problem is that Islam, like Judaism before it, construes the divine as a Lord whose absolute will stands in an external relation to humanity. Jehovah and Allah are both one and infinite *only*, remaining in the sheer transcendence of absolute Lordship. Humanity may be created in the image of God and indeed comprise the only image that the purely spiritual divine can have, at least terrestrially.[98] Yet, humanity relates

---

95 Slavery sanctioned by officially governing *Shariah* law persisted in the Ottoman Empire and Persia early into the twentieth century and until 1962 in Yemen and Saudi Arabia. See Lewis, *What Went Wrong?*, p. 89.

96 Although in 1856 the Ottoman Empire abolished the *jizya* poll tax and the ban on non-Muslims bearing arms, the prohibitions remained banning non-Muslims from Arabia and marriage between non-Muslim men and Muslim women. See Lewis, *What Went Wrong?*, p. 91.

97 This is true of efforts, such as those of Muhammad Taha (executed in 1985 for apostasy by the Sudanese rulers) and his protégé An-Na'im, to limit the conflict of *Shariah* with human rights by treating Koranic passages and *sunnahs* from Muhammad's time in Medina as transitional strictures applying only to that precarious interim situation. Although this strategy may bound these strictures' jurisdiction, it does not question the public authority of Islamic holy law in general. See David Herbert, *Religion and Civil Society: Rethinking Public Religion in the Contemporary World* (Aldershot, UK: Ashgate, 2003) pp. 145–6.

98 Religion must confront the possibility of non-human extraterrestrial forms of intelligent life, which can just as well be in the image of a spiritualized divine.

to Allah, as it does to Jehovah, as mere human subjects, submitting in utter servitude to external commands requiring positive actions. On this basis, achieving oneness with God depends upon fulfilling one or another divine commandment, rather than engaging in any self-legislating moral or political activity.[99] This reflects the abstract character of the denaturalization common to Jehovah and Allah. Both stand apart from their creation, such that the sovereignty of the divine over everything natural still presents an abiding distinction leaving the infinity of God tainted by a limit—the externality of the finite. Accordingly, as much as the pure will of Jehovah and Allah implies the freedom of a humanity created in its image, humanity still stands subject to positive prescriptions that are external to self-determination. This contradictory predicament is reflected in the abject prostration of Muslim prayer, where the faithful bow down to the ground before Allah as veritable slaves of God,[100] and, more significantly, in the widespread traditional acceptance of predestination and of the inscrutability of divine will, whose commands are regarded to be beyond any determination by reason.

The basic Muslim prescriptions on diet, washing, ritual prayer, and pilgrimage may all be as inoffensive to the rights of individuals as the corresponding sacred commands on Jews and Sikhs, but these prescriptions do lack any inherent rationality and any inherent recognition of how self-determination involves submission to self-legislation. Nevertheless, just as Judaism has reformed itself to render strict ritual observance unessential to belief, so Islam can undergo similar self-reinterpretation without abandoning the basic sovereignty of Allah and the universal character of Muslim faith. The infinitude of the divine can hardly be impeached by alterations or neglect of ritual conventions, particularly when fixating upon such tangible behavior falls perilously close to idolatry.[101] Nor does the universal appeal of Islam suffer when specific rituals are ignored,

---

99   Fackenheim makes these points, following Hegel, with reference to Judaism, but they all can be extended, as done here, to Islam. See Emil Fackenheim, *The Religious Dimension in Hegel's Thought* (Boston: Beacon Press, 1967), pp. 134–6. In the addition to paragraph 112 of the *Logic*, Hegel does observe that "to look at God ... as the Lord, and the Lord alone, is especially characteristic of Judaism and also of Mohammedanism." See G.W.F. Hegel, *Logic: Being Part One of the Encyclopaedia of the Philosophical Sciences*, trans. William Wallace (Oxford: Oxford University Press, 1975), p. 164.

100   See George Anastaplo, *But Not Philosophy*, p. 185.

101   As Gibbon points out, the rituals that pilgrims observe in visiting Mecca and Medina largely derive from the practices of the pre-Islamic Arabian

especially when they are alien to local customs and have no necessary connection to finding one's truth in an absolute Lord and Creator. If anything, absolutizing any such arbitrary practices binds the command of Allah to forms of obedience that should have no more value for the divine than any other conventions of piety. Averroes's call for rational reinterpretation can here find ready application.

Meeting the challenge of predestination and the absolute hegemony of holy law is another matter, requiring more than such piecemeal reinterpretation. Whatever one's view of ritual conventions, predestination and the exclusivity of *Shariah* both plausibly appear to be absolutely vital elements of Islamic faith.

If predestination is denied, how can Allah retain the character of being the absolute Lord, whose will both creates and governs creation? Any allowance of personal freedom seems to introduce a limit to divine power. Yet, if humanity is created in the image of Allah, how can humans be deprived of responsibility for their own conduct? If our lives are predestined, then not only do we show little resemblance to the divine, but evil must be attributed to Allah. Complicating matters is that conflicting Koranic texts give apparent support to both sides,[102] affording devout supporters of free will like the Qadarites as much scriptural backing as their opposing Jabriya advocates of blind fatalism.[103]

The Augustinian solution to the problem of evil[104] provides an answer as fundamentally amenable to Islam as to Christianity: creation is all the more perfect for including individuals who have a will of their own, for a creation lacking free beings is more deficient than one in which individuals have choice and the ability to perform good deeds. Moreover, allowance of free will and personal responsibility makes evil comprehensible by taking it

---

idolaters. See Edward Gibbon, *The Decline and Fall of the Roman Empire: Volume III*, pp. 1730–31.

102   As Anastaplo points out, passages such as "Truth comes from your Lord. Let anyone who will, believe, and let anyone who wishes, disbelieve" (18:29) affirm free will, whereas others, such as "God lets anyone He wishes go astray while He guides whoever he wishes" (35:8), describe Allah as all-determining. See Anastaplo, *But Not Philosophy*, p. 201.

103   For a brief account of the Qadarites, see Ibn Warraq, *Why I Am Not A Muslim*, p. 245.

104   Saint Augustine gives the classic formulation of his solution in *On Free Choice of the Will*, trans. Thomas Williams (Indianapolis: Hackett Publishing, 1993).

out of God's hands, while eliminating the specter of Manichean dualism,[105] which undermines the infinity of the divine by opposing polar forces of good and evil. Further, acknowledgment of human free will makes it intelligible for the divine to issue commands, which, unlike physical laws, may or may not be obeyed, depending upon the choices of individuals.[106]

Supplanting predestination with acknowledgement of freedom and responsibility may be crucial for enabling revealed religion to be internally coherent as well as in accord with right, but it does not of itself resolve the problem presented by holy law. Individuals may have free will, but that capacity does not give them any *right* to self-legislation so long as God is presumed to be politically sovereign, issuing commands requiring positive obedience, commands regarded to be the exclusive source of binding law. With *Shariah* in force, imposing Allah's sovereignty, there can be no government of, by, and for the people. Self-government is precluded, for if law is holy, it is made by God and not by the citizenry.

On face value, the political sovereignty of Allah makes clear sense if one subscribes to the basic message of Muhammad. If God is the all powerful and perfect Lord of creation, divine commands should provide the rule of life by which humanity attains its true essence. Revelation provides humanity with those commands, which therefore should reign supreme thanks to rulers who govern in the name of God by implementing the commands that revelation already contains. Judges may be necessary to determine how to apply these divine laws to particular cases, but no new legislation is necessary, both because divine law should be considered perfect and complete, and because no human legislative power could enjoy any unconditionally binding authority. If Islam were not a revealed religion, divine commands would not be available and believers would be left relying upon their own reason and prudence to decide under what laws to live. Since, however, the Prophet is the messenger of divine will, holy law has been revealed and our religious obligation is none other than to insure that *Shariah* governs all human affairs. Interpretation may be enrolled to determine what individual holy laws mean, but that interpretive

---

105   Saint Augustine describes his own flirtation with and subsequent repudiation of Manicheanism in his *Confessions*, trans. R.S. Pine-Coffin (Harmondsworth, UK: Penguin, 1961), Book VII, Chs 2–5, pp. 135–9.

106   Admittedly, this still leaves difficulties *if* one must also allow for an infinite divine Grace. As Fackenheim observes, that allowance would seem to leave little place for any freedom, just as human freedom seems to leave no place for a divine Grace, which must be passively received without regard for personal responsibility. See *The Religious Dimension in Hegel's Thought*, p. 196.

endeavor presupposes that their identity and absolute hegemony is beyond interpretation.

The Caliphate combination of highest religious and political authority would accordingly best insure not only that holy law rules supreme, but that its implementation takes place without debilitating competition between those who best understand the divine word and those empowered to execute it.

Moreover, by uniting religion and political power, the Caliphate gives the Muslim empire an additional force that other regimes lack. As Ibn Khaldûn argues in *The Muqaddimah*,[107] although all regimes depend upon group feeling for their power, when religious coloring is absent, group feeling is more susceptible to erosion. Without devotion to a common religious truth, the conflicting diversity of worldly interests and false purposes elicits jealousy, envy, and the collapse of solidarity. A regime whose power rests upon submission to religious authority escapes this disunity and therefore possesses a more durable group feeling, enabling it to prevail over larger nations, whose members are more likely to abandon one another in fear of death.

Admittedly, sustaining the unity of religious and political authority may become unfeasible due to the sheer expanse of the *Dar al Islam* and the challenge of defending it against the *Dar al Harb* and absorbing the latter into the empire of Islam. On the one hand, as Ibn Khaldûn explained in 1377,[108] expanding conquest at some point will exhaust the numerical strength of the Caliphate's supporters, whereas the growing empire will find it increasingly difficult to incorporate more and more tribes and peoples due to the differences in their opinions and desires. Even then, it will make sense to retain a Caliphate that is recognized as the highest religious authority for all Islam, so that independent Muslim rulers can uphold *Shariah* in their realms without setting Islam against itself in the internecine conflict that plagued Christendom during the centuries of religious war between Protestants and Catholics. In this respect, the political sovereignty of Allah can be established in individual Muslim states, all paying homage to the Caliphate, just as Stalin sought to have socialism erected in one nation at a time, while maintaining the world

---

107   Ibn Khaldûn, *The Muqaddimah: An Introduction to History*, trans. Franz Rosenthal, ed. and abridged by N.J. Dawood (Princeton, NJ: Princeton University Press, 1967), pp. 125–6.

108   Ibn Khaldûn, *The Muqaddimah*, pp. 130–31.

revolutionary authority of the Comintern.[109] Along these lines, Muhammad Iqbāl, the intellectual forerunner of the creation of Pakistan, argued that in the modern world the only feasible way to uphold the rule of *Shariah* was within separate Islamic states.[110] Of course, Muslim multinationalism can be contested, as it was by al-Afghānī, the Islamist Trotsky, who argued in the late nineteenth century that the decline of Islam was due to its political fragmentation, and that only a united and all-embracing Islam could resist infidel aggression and reconquer lost territories of the *Dār al-Islam*.[111]

In face of any of these lines of argument, how can *Shariah* possibly be made a private matter, separating religion and rule? Would this not repudiate the truth of revelation and violate divine command, not only by treating it as non-obligatory, but by capitulating to a secular law-making power that lacks authority? Indeed, is not this separation of religion and state the fundamental abomination of the United States, which Usama bin Laden purportedly denounces in his "letter to America", published in November 2002, declaiming, "You are the nation who, rather than ruling by the *Shariah* of Allah in its Constitution and Laws, choose to invent your own laws as you will and desire ... contradicting the pure nature which affirms Absolute Authority to the Lord and your Creator?"[112]

To respond to these questions and enable Islam to become compatible with modern freedom without forfeiting all claim to truth, one must take seriously the fundamental proviso of all religion, that humanity find its true essence in its relation to the divine. Ultimately, for this to be possible, humanity must find itself in relating to the divine, just as the divine must relate to itself in being related to by humanity. Otherwise the immanent connection between the divine and humanity is wanting and religion is in vain. The spiritualized Lord of Islam can be the truth of humanity to the degree that humanity's true nature resides in free will. Humanity can be in the image of Allah only insofar as we are defined above all by the same freedom that characterizes the absolute volition of the divine.

---

109 The idea of sovereign nation states thus need not be completely incompatible with belief in the sovereignty of Allah, contra Huntington. Nevertheless, it is noteworthy, as Huntington observes, that today only Islamic nations "have interstate organizations with memberships based on religion" (for example the Organization of the Islamic Conference). See Huntington, *The Clash of Civilizations and the Remaking of World Order*, pp. 175–6.

110 Ahmad, *Studies in Islamic Culture in the Indian Environment*, p. 272.

111 See Ahmad, *Studies in Islamic Culture in the Indian Environment*, pp. 61–2.

112 Lewis, *The Crisis of Islam*, p. 159.

Only by being fundamentally what we will ourselves to be can we exhibit the same independence from given nature that characterizes Allah as creator of the cosmos. Consequently, the law of Allah that provides us with our true guidance can only be a rule of self-guidance, a law of freedom. For this reason, the Koranic saying that there is "No compulsion in religion" (2:256) is of fundamental importance for freeing Islam of its Caliphate deformation.[113] True religion cannot be compulsory. It can no more make its believers slaves of God, than make God a tyrant. For humanity to find its truth in the divine and for the divine to be conscious of itself in the devotion of its faithful, belief must be voluntarily adopted and the content of belief must acknowledge the truth of emancipation. Accordingly, neither apostasy nor blasphemy can be punishable offenses. Nor can sanctions be imposed upon belief in religions that subject humanity to rules of spiritual oppression. Such beliefs may be deplorable, but the most that one can permissibly do is try to convince such believers of the ultimate error of such faiths and give them an opportunity to voluntarily subscribe to a religious credo providing a true conception of humanity. Accordingly, religious law must itself have a purely voluntary jurisdiction, depending upon its voluntary acceptance by the faithful. Moreover, its laws must either be rules of freedom or rules of devotional behavior that violate no rights of either believers or non-believers.

Making this argument as a theological imperative completely internal to Islam is fundamentally supported by the basic spirituality of Allah, by which the divine is construed as standing over and against nature as creator and absolute Lord, and more specifically, as creator of humanity in the image of God. By themselves, these basic tenants give ample support to the understanding that genuine holy law can only be a law a freedom, fully compatible with the privatization of religion required by the emancipation of modernity. Supported by Averroes's insight that true revelation cannot conflict with philosophical truth, Islam can consistently proceed with the allegorical reinterpretations necessary to take to the heart of faith the exclusive normativity of self-determination established by the philosophical critique of foundationalism. By acknowledging the

---

113   Of course, what matters is how this verse is interpreted. As Lewis points out, Muslim jurists and rulers traditionally interpreted it to allow limited toleration of other religious beliefs, but only so far as the primacy of Islam and the supremacy of Muslims within the *Dar al Islam* were not challenged. See Lewis, *What Went Wrong?*, p. 113.

truth of freedom's legitimacy, Islam can embrace the privatization of faith without succumbing to an enfeebling relativism.

If instead, Islam upholds *Shariah* as a law of compulsory bondage, where the sovereignty of the citizenry is usurped by the claimants of the sovereignty of Allah, Islam cannot coherently defend the truth of its alleged revelation. Like any creed that makes conduct legitimate by being determined not by itself but by something alien, Islam will fall into the fatal trap of foundational justification. With what confers validity separate from what enjoys validity, the source of justification can never satisfy its own validity requirement. For if the foundation of validity is to enjoy the legitimacy it confers on what it grounds, that foundation will cease to determine something other than itself, and will instead revert to what is self-determined. This is ultimately why the divine cannot be accorded goodness simply for whatever it wills. That would be the highest embrace of foundational justification—where what is valid is valid only because it has the right source. Instead, Allah must will what is good to be the all-perfect divine and the only coherently justifiable good is self-determination.

To redeem itself on purely theological grounds, Islam must therefore undertake the same recognition of religious freedom and ecumenical toleration that entails jettisoning the identification of Islam with rule fostered by canonizing the historical career of Muhammad and his imperial successors. These paths of religious reformation are far from untraveled, as the lives of modernized Muslims can testify, both by way of private example and in courageous public resistance to Islamist zealots in and out of power.[114] The struggle to make these paths the predominant self-interpretation of Islam will determine whether the Muslim faith can be at home in the modern world and true to what is of ultimate value to humanity.[115]

---

114 As Lewis points out, although most contemporary terrorists are Islamists, most Muslims are not Islamists and most Islamists are not engaged in terrorism. See Lewis, *The Crisis of Islam*, p. 135.

115 The very possibility of this struggle for the reformation of Islam is what refutes Huntington's claim that "The underlying problem for the West is not Islamic fundamentalism. It is Islam, a different civilization whose people are convinced of the superiority of their culture and are obsessed with the inferiority of their power." That same possibility of religious reform equally undermines Huntington's correlative claim that "The problem for Islam is ... the West, a different civilization whose people are convinced of the universality of their culture and believe that their superior, if declining, power imposes on them the obligation to extend that culture throughout the world." (Huntington, *The Clash of Civilizations and the Remaking of World Order*, pp. 217–18). So long as Islam

What makes this theological struggle especially challenging is that it must predominantly take place in post-colonial nations, burdened by pre-modern traditions, the deformations of colonial exploitation, and the inequalities between self-modernized and externally modernized countries. The promise of modern institutions of freedom continues to be tainted by the bleak reality of the post-colonial condition, where the new secular order progressively strangling traditional relations offers a society of dubious promise. Whether mouthing the ideals of Jefferson or Marx, the new post-colonial regime is one in which the widening gulf of its own rich and poor and between itself and the "first" world overwhelms efforts to secure equal economic opportunity, puts enormous destructive pressures on marital and parental relations, and undercuts the ability of government to escape widespread corruption, political inequality, outright dictatorship, and subservience of its economy, culture, and government policy to foreign influence. These are conditions that give allure to abandoning the project of modern emancipation. On the one hand, they fuel the proto-fascist alternative of the ethnic political solidarity of Pan-Arab movements and their counterparts, which draw on post-modern ideologies affirming the particular at the expense of the universal. On the other hand, they encourage nostalgia for the pre-modern moorings of Islamist theocracy.

Indeed, the persistence of secular autocracies in the post-colonial world fosters the rise of Islamist reaction for two crucial reasons.[116] On the one hand, the political oppression and social injustice of secular despotisms discredits the whole project of modernity to which secular nationalists and socialists claim allegiance. On the other hand, the repressions of secular regimes greatly weaken, if not entirely eliminate, secular opposition groups, be they political parties or voluntary organizations in civil society.[117] In Muslim nations, this leaves the only organized alternative Islamic religious organizations, whose vast network of mosques, madrasas,

---

is dominated by the unreformed Caliphate thinking of Islamist zealotry, it will oppose not just the self-modernized West, but the modernity that is fast rising in the East, most spectacularly with respect to civil society, and more unevenly with respect to the institutions of self-government.

116   Huntington observes that Islamist strength "was weaker in countries, such as Morocco and Turkey, that allowed some degree of multiparty competition than it was in countries that suppressed all opposition." See Huntington, *The Clash of Civilizations and the Remaking of World Order*, p. 115.

117   Lewis observes that reform and modernization reinforce autocracy by undermining traditional intermediary powers, which helps explain the rise of secular dictators in the first place. See Lewis, *What Went Wrong?*, p. 53.

and pious foundations (*waqf*)[118] provides unobstructed opportunities for regular meetings and popular mobilizations that no other group can match.[119] Not only are secular tyrants at pains to control what Muslim clerics preach in mosques and madrasas, but it is precisely the Islamist fanatics who will give these religious institutions a political mission and use them as fulcrums for seizing power. Because more emancipated Muslims will not even want to use mosques as political instruments, the field is open for Islamist reaction to commandeer the only organized movement that secular tyrants have not strangled.[120]

Consequently, any democratic transformation permitting religious parties to contest elections must face the prospect of Islamists imposing their theocratic tyranny by the same electoral niceties that allowed Hitler to initiate his thousand year *Reich*.[121] Although supporters of democratic process may feel obliged to give every political opportunity to Islamist parties, ignoring how religious parties are inherently anti-democratic, the scruples of Islamists can hardly permit them to relinquish the sovereignty of Allah once it has been established through their electoral success.[122] For this reason, as Bernard Lewis presciently observes, free and fair elections cannot *inaugurate* democratization in Muslim nations where Islamist movements are the primary organized opposition to secular autocrats.[123]

This is true even if religious parties are banned from vying for power and even if Islam is deprived of the stifling cultural hegemony that discourages secular artists, scientists, scholars, philosophers, labor leaders, business figures, and voluntary groups in civil society from contesting *Shariah* regimentation. The "democratization" of Islamic nations will still provide no abiding solution if it does not address the

---

118   Although modernizing autocrats may have put the *waqfs* under state control (Lewis, *What Went Wrong?*, p. 111), they still exist and provide an institutional springboard for Islamist zealots.

119   Lewis discusses this organizational advantage in *The Crisis of Islam*, pp. 23, 133.

120   If it were not for the Islamist commandeering of Muslim religious institutions, secular despotism otherwise might clear the way for democracy, since, as Walzer points out, it levels the political universe by destroying existing intermediate powers embodied in feudal, clan, tribal, and regional allegiances. Walzer, *Revolution of the Saints*, p. 151.

121   The electoral policy of Islamist theocrats has been classically formulated as "One man (men only), one vote, once." See Lewis, *The Crisis of Islam*, p. 112.

122   Lewis, *The Crisis of Islam*, pp. 111–12.

123   Lewis, *The Crisis of Islam*, p. 112.

household and social inequalities that undercut real equal political participation. Universal suffrage and monitored elections may eliminate the stranglehold of royal families, tribal despots, and secular tyrants. Yet so long as patriarchy at home constricts women's engagement in society and politics, so long as the divide of rich and poor facilitates the disproportionate electoral influence of the economically powerful, and so long as that divide encourages the rampant corruption of public officials that subverts the integrity of government, the formalities of democratic process will only mask the triumph of oligarchy over self-rule.

These problems require more than a domestic solution, for the liabilities of the post-colonial situation leave Muslim nations in such disadvantage relative to the self-modernized first world that "free trade" and benign neglect only threaten to exacerbate the disparities that block opportunity in every sphere of right. International initiatives to promote more equitable capital accumulation and the provision of the social prerequisites for equal economic opportunity must, however, contend with the obstacles posed by the sovereign independence of post-colonial nations. Although that independence provides them some room for maneuver to minimize foreign domination, it equally entails that any international remedies to global inequities must find their way past the corruption and autocratic license of ruling regimes.

Overcoming these conditions may not guarantee the self-modernization of Islam, but it would be illusory to think that the war on terrorism can succeed unless these barriers to religious reform are no less attended to than combating the holy warriors by arms as well as theological reinterpretation. Doing so is not merely a pragmatic strategy. Alleviating the post-colonial condition is itself an imperative of the principles of modernity, an imperative whose fulfillment secures the globalization of the institutions of freedom against which religious reaction rebels.

Works Cited

Adorno, Theodor W., *Philosophy of Modern Music*, trans. Anne G. Mitchell and Wesley V. Blomster (New York: Continuum, 1994).

Ahmad, Aziz, *Studies in Islamic Culture in the Indian Environment* (New Delhi: Oxford University Press, 1964).

Algazali, *Deliverance From Error* and *The Incoherence of the Philosophers*, selections trans. G. F. Hourani, in *Philosophy in the Middle Ages, Second Edition*, ed. Arthur Hyman and James J. Walsh (Indianapolis: Hackett Publishing, 1986).

Anastaplo, George, *But Not Philosophy* (Lanham, MD: Lexington Books, 2002).

Arendt, Hannah, *Essays in Understanding 1930–1954*, ed. Jerome Kohn (New York: Harcourt Brace & Company, 1994).

Arendt, Hannah, *The Human Condition* (Chicago: The University of Chicago Press, 1958).

Arendt, Hannah, *The Origins of Totalitarianism* (New York: Harcourt Brace Jovanovich, 1973).

Augustine, Saint, *Confessions*, trans. R.S. Pine-Coffin (Harmondsworth, UK: Penguin, 1961).

Augustine, Saint, *On Free Choice of the Will*, trans. Thomas Williams (Indianapolis: Hackett, 1993).

Averroes, *The Decisive Treatise Determining the Nature of the Connection Between Religion and Philosophy*, trans. G.F. Hourani, in *Philosophy in the Middle Ages, Second Edition*, ed. Arthur Hyman and James J. Walsh (Indianapolis: Hackett Publishing, 1986).

Badiou, Alain, *Infinite Thought: Truth and the Return of Philosophy*, trans. Oliver Feltham and Justin Clemens (London: Continuum, 2004).

Dupré, Louis, *A Dubious Heritage: Studies in the Philosophy of Religion after Kant* (New York: Paulist Press, 1977).

Fackenheim, Emil, *The Religious Dimension in Hegel's Thought* (Boston: Beacon Press, 1967).

Foster, Michael B., "The Christian Doctrine of Creation and the Rise of Modern Natural Science" (*Mind*, vol. XLIII, 1934).

Foucault, Michel, *Discipline and Punish: The Birth of the Prison*, trans. Alan Sheridan (New York: Vintage Books: 1979).

Gibbon, Edward, *The Decline and Fall of the Roman Empire: Volume III* (New York: Heritage Press, 1946).

Hegel, G.W.F., *Elements of the Philosophy of Right*, trans. H.B. Nisbet (Cambridge: Cambridge University Press, 1991).

Hegel, G.W.F., *Lectures on the Philosophy of Religion: One Volume Edition, The Lectures of 1827*, ed. Peter Hodgson, trans. R.F. Brown, P.C. Hodgson, and J.M. Stewart with assistance of H.S. Harris (Berkeley: University of California Press, 1988).

Hegel, G.W.F., *Logic: Being Part One of the Encyclopaedia of the Philosophical Sciences*, trans. William Wallace (Oxford: Oxford University Press, 1975).

Hegel, G.W.F., *The Philosophy of History*, trans. J. Sibree (New York: Dover Publications, 1956).

Heidegger, Martin, *Basic Writings*, ed. David Farrell Krell (New York: Harper Collins, 1993).

Herbert, David, *Religion and Civil Society: Rethinking Public Religion in the Contemporary World* (Aldershot, UK: Ashgate, 2003).

Holy Bible – King James Version (New York: American Bible Society, 1967).

Horkheimer, Max and Adorno, Theodor W., *Dialectic of the Enlightenment: Philosophical Fragments*, trans. Edmund Jephcott (Stanford, CA: Stanford University Press, 1992).

Houlgate, Stephen, *An Introduction to Hegel: Freedom, Truth and History* (Oxford: Blackwell Publishing, 2005).

Huntington, Samuel P., *The Clash of Civilizations and the Remaking of World Order* (New York: Simon and Schuster Paperbacks, 2003).

Kant, Immanuel, *The Metaphysics of Morals*, trans. Mary Gregor (New York: Cambridge University Press, 1991).

Kant, Immanuel, *Religion Within the Limits of Reason Alone*, trans. Theodore M. Greene and Hoyt H. Hudson (New York: Harper & Row, 1960).

Khaldûn, Ibn, *The Muqaddimah: An Introduction to History*, trans. Franz Rosenthal, ed. and abridged by N.J. Dawood (Princeton, NJ: Princeton Unversity Press, 1967).

Kierkegaard, Søren, *Concluding Unscientific Postscript*, trans. David F. Swenson and Walter Lowrie (Princeton, NJ: Princeton University Press, 1968).

Koran, trans. N.J. Dawood (London: Penguin Books, 1999).

Lewis, Bernard, *The Crisis of Islam: Holy War and Unholy Terror* (New York: Random House, 2004).

Lewis, Bernard, *What Went Wrong? Western Impact and Middle Eastern Response* (New York: Oxford University Press, 2002).

Lukács, Georg, *The Theory of the Novel*, trans. Anna Bostock (Cambridge, MA: MIT Press, 1971).

Luxemburg, Rosa, *The Accumulation of Capital*, trans. Agnes Schwarzschild (New York: Monthly Review Press, 1968).

MacIntyre, Alasdair, *After Virtue* (Notre Dame, IN: University of Notre Dame Press, 1981).

Maker, William, *Philosophy Without Foundations: Rethinking Hegel* (Albany: State University of New York Press, 1994).

Mango, Andrew, *Atatürk: The Biography of the Founder of Modern Turkey* (Woodstock and New York: The Overlook Press, 2002).

Marx, Karl, *Capital – Volume I*, trans. Samuel Moore and Edward Aveling (New York: International Publishers, 1967).

Marx, Karl, *Early Writings*, trans. T.B. Bottomore (New York: McGraw Hill, 1964).

Marx, Karl, *Karl Marx on Colonialism and Modernization*, ed. Shlomo Avineri (New York: Anchor Books, 1968).

Mill, John Stuart, *Considerations on Representative Government*, in John Stuart Mill, *Three Essays* (Oxford: Oxford University Press, 1987).

Naipaul, V.S., *Beyond Belief: Islamic Excursions Among the Converted Peoples* (New York: Vintage International, 1998).

Oakeshott, Michael, *On Human Conduct* (Oxford: Oxford University Press, 1975).

Plato, *Complete Works*, ed. John Cooper (Indianapolis: Hackett Publishing Company, 1997).

Rorty, Richard, *Contingency, Irony, and Solidarity* (Cambridge: Cambridge University Press, 1989).

Rousseau, Jean-Jacques, *The Social Contract and other later political writings*, ed. Victor Gourevitch (Cambridge: Cambridge University Press, 1997).

Schacht, Joseph and C. E. Bosworth, *The Legacy of Islam* (Oxford: Oxford University Press, 1964).

Spinoza, Benedict de, *The Complete Works*, trans. Samuel Shirley, ed. Michael L. Morgan (Indianapolis: Hackett Publishing Company, 2002).

Strauss, Leo, *Jewish Philosophy and the Crisis of Modernity: Essays and Lectures in Modern Jewish Thought*, ed. Kenneth Hart Green (Albany: State University of New York Press, 1997).

Tocqueville, Alexis de, *De La Démocratie en Amérique* (Paris: Garnier-Flammarion, 1981).

Walzer, Michael, *Arguing about War* (New Haven, CT: Yale University Press, 2004).

Walzer, Michael, *Exodus and Revolution* (New York: Basic Books, 1985).

Walzer, Michael, *The Revolution of the Saints: A Study in the Origins of Radical Politics* (Cambridge, MA: Harvard University Press, 1982).

Warraq, Ibn, *Why I Am Not A Muslim* (Amherst, NY: Prometheus Books, 1995).

Winfield, Richard Dien, *From Concept to Objectivity: Thinking Through Hegel's Subjective Logic* (Aldershot, UK: Ashgate, 2006).

Winfield, Richard Dien, *Stylistics: Rethinking the Art Forms After Hegel* (Albany: State University of New York Press, 1996).

Winfield, Richard Dien, *Systematic Aesthetics* (Gainesville: University Press of Florida, 1995).

Winfield, Richard Dien, *The Just Economy* (London: Routledge, 1988).

Winfield, Richard Dien, *The Just State: Rethinking Self-Government* (Amherst, NY: Humanity Books, 2005).

Index